1988

Painting Animals
in Watercolor

Painting animals in watercolor

SALLY MICHEL

WATSON-GUPTHILL PUBLICATIONS
NEW YORK

Copyright © Search Press Ltd

First published 1985 in the United States and Canada by
Watson-Gupthill Publications, a division of Billboard
Publications, Inc., 1515 Broadway, New York, N.Y. 10036.

First Printing, 1985

Library of Congress Catalog Card Number: 85-40596

Text, drawings and paintings by Sally Michel
Design by David Stanley

ISBN 0 8230 3559 X

Manufactured in Spain

Made and printed in Spain by A. G. Elkar, S. Coop.
Bilbao-12 - D. L. BI-226-82

CONTENTS

INTRODUCTION

Introduction

One essential difference between painting or drawing animals and painting or drawing other subjects — landscapes, still lifes, plants, buildings, or even a human portrait — is that, while most of these stay reasonably still, animals move. When you start to draw a motionless and apparently sleeping animal, it is impossible to know whether you will have time for a detailed, leisurely study, or will need to work very fast to sketch its general appearance.

Another difference is that a subjective approach, appropriate to most other subjects, will probably defeat its own object in the case of animal painting. There is no point in painting an animal if you are not going to present its essential character, whether in near-photographic detail or as a swiftly observed and recorded impression. This requires considerable accuracy — for if the structure is not right, your drawing will not be of that animal. This is not to say that careful observation and accurate drawing are less important for other subjects, but there is more scope for choice and selection. For instance, a tree in a landscape or an awkward spray of leaves in a flower painting can be moved to improve the composition. And television antennae and parked cars can be omitted from the picture of a cottage. All this is permissable, even desirable. But, with animals, alteration may mean that you have created a new animal or misrepresented an existing one.

Even the apparently random patches of color on a tortoiseshell cat obey certain rules, and the position of feet depends on the position of the other parts of the animal. Obviously some changes can be made, but enormous care must be taken to see that there is a good reason for each. The danger of making arbitrary alterations is greater with wild animals than with domestic pets. If you change the pattern on a giraffe shown in a particular landscape, you may be transporting a particular variety many hundreds of miles from its native habitat, and making its camouflage ineffectual in addition!

For most of us, however, more opportunities arise for drawing and painting domestic animals, and experience gained from working on these can be applied to any other creatures we may become interested in.

This book begins with a discussion of the general approach to the subject: what to do, how to start, and what to use; how to reconcile ability with ambition, maintain enjoyment, and avoid discouragement.

Next comes the range of accessible subjects. I make no apology for including a large section on dogs, which are so varied in size and shape. Cats, the other principal sharers of our home life, also have a chapter of their own. I then look at birds and other small creatures that live in our homes — for example, gerbils, guinea pigs, hamsters, and fish.

Finally we turn to horses and other animals found outside our homes, in gardens, the countryside, parks and zoos — both as subjects of portraits and as elements in a larger scene.

Anyone interested in the subject of animal painting in watercolor probably already has some familiarity with the medium, so it seems superfluous to expatiate on the character and qualities of watercolor or to give long lists of pigments and describe the available brushes, papers, and other materials, except in regard to the particular requirements of painting animals. It may be worth emphasizing, however, that it is best to use materials of good quality and to pay attention to the permanence of pigments. The more expensive "Artist's" watercolors go further than cheaper grades, though even they vary in permanence; earth colors are among the most stable. Good brushes last longer than inferior ones, but sable can be prohibitively expensive. Good-quality nylon brushes can be excellent, beautifully springy when new, although some have a tendency to change suddenly into a kind of miniature whisk broom. Nevertheless, the larger sizes are so much cheaper than their sable equivalents that one or two are worth buying. They are harder than sable, but this may be preferable to some of the other less expensive large wash brushes in camel's hair, which are floppy and soft. It is a matter of personal preference.

The particular requirements for animal work are:
1. Plenty of paper for preliminary drawings. You need to be able to use it without worrying about the cost, as you want to record every movement and position of the animal to refer to when making your picture.
2. A small, light drawing board — a piece of plywood about 12 in. × 16 in. (30 cm × 40 cm) is a good size. This can be useful when you are pursuing a reluctant model as it retreats from view, or takes up a position behind furniture to keep an eye on you and your questionable activities.
3. One or two really fine brushes, no. 0 or 00, for the details of hair and whiskers.
4. If you intend to paint mammals, colors that will permit you to mix a wide range of browns, from pale yellowish, to reddish, to dark. In effect, this means much the same palette as for most other subjects, but with perhaps a larger choice of browns. As with any painting medium, it is a good idea to start with a small selection of six to eight pigments and add to these if you find you are lacking a color. You also need everything you might want for landscape, as the backgrounds will often be precisely that.

Colors and treatment

I find that the colors I use most are:
Yellow ocher
Burnt sienna
A very sharp lemon yellow (Winsor yellow or cadmium lemon)
Lamp black
Phthalocyanine blue
Payne's gray.

Some others that are almost equally essential, but used in smaller amounts, are:
Cadmium red light
Permanent rose (for tongues, noses and toes, particularly for white or very young animals)
A deeper yellow — cadmium (*not* chrome yellow, which fades)
French ultramarine
Winsor violet (particularly useful for the more subtle browns of fur and feathers).

Incidentally, when you paint tropical birds or fish, they are so brilliant that it may be necessary to use specially bought colors.

The pictures on pages 10 – 13 show different approaches, ranging in complexity from a very simple black and white cat to the peacock butterfly on page 12. The cat is little more than a one-color wash drawing, with small additions for the features. The hedgehog was first drawn in pencil, with washes added, and the rooster drawn in pen, with washes added. The squirrel was built up in loose, wet washes on wet paper; the details were then sharpened and many hairs added with a fine brush. The badger was treated in much the same way, but in a simpler, broader style.

Watercolor techniques

The pony here was built up with a wet wash, one part at a time. When they were dry, the parts were coordinated with a pale wash, which preserved their definition and gave an impression of the glossiness of the pony's hide. The tail, mane, and grass were added as separate patches of color to complete the sketch.

The peacock butterfly is the most complex of these sketches — both the insect itself and the flower on which it has settled. The butterfly's markings demand a detailed and realistic treatment, and this dictates the style of the flower, which needs to be consistent with the rest.

The treatment used for the fox is fairly complicated, combining elements used in the badger and pony sketches. It is a particularly useful approach for animals and is employed in many of the pictures in this book. I have included some of my previous fox sketches, which helped me in building up the picture.

These pictures are here to illustrate techniques. They are not necessarily the most suitable subjects for a

beginner to start with. Instead, because of the inherent problem of a moving model, it is sensible to start with a sleeping subject. It may not stay asleep, and even if it does, it may still move; but the chances are that there will be periods when you can proceed uninterrupted.

Drawing as a basis for watercolor

Sleeping dogs: *the drawings on these two pages, the product of one session, show how even a sleeping dog can provide a variety of poses.*

Whatever painting medium you intend to use, you must start with drawing. After years of experience, an artist may base his picture on a sketch so apparently slight that it seems as if the drawing stage were being by-passed. For this to be done successfully, careful study and observation must have been carried out in the past, over many years. It is the artist's thorough knowledge of the subject that enables him to sum up very quickly the essential facts of the model before him, add these to what is already in his memory, and produce an accurate presentation of what is there. Until this knowledge has been gained, you should spend as much time as you can on drawing and on the careful exploratory looking that is its necessary preliminary and accompaniment. Even if you have no immediate intention of doing a painting, no time spent on drawing is wasted. Carry a sketchbook with you and draw whenever possible. Practice in draw-ing, with any subject, increases your ability to draw any other subject. Even if the result appears to be of little significance, the process adds to your general ability. By filling sketch-books with drawings of many different animals, you are building your knowledge of their struc-ture and habits, as well as a useful record to refer to for later work. Do not be disheartened at the apparent im-possibility of completing any one drawing — even the smallest sketch can be useful. Start another drawing if your subject moves — later you may well have a chance to go back to the first one. Keep all your drawings, however incomplete; make written notes about colors, behavior, the age and sex of the animal, and anything else that contributes to your knowledge. Label and date all your drawings, and don't forget to include the year. Try to draw from different viewpoints, and pay atten-tion to the structure of eyes, feet, and ears.

Eyes, ears, feet, and hooves

In drawing and painting animals, it is essential to have some knowledge of the structural principles of certain features and details. This enables you to draw them with understanding and to compare the features in different animals, to perceive how they are the same and how they differ.

In all vertebrates, for instance, the eyes are more or less spherical, which means that the surface of the visible part is curved. The part that is not visible affects the shape of the face around the eye, and it can often be detected where these forms continue the rounded shape of the whole eye, where bone forms a protective curve around it, and where eyelids follow its shape.

The visible part of the eye is not always the same: humans show a lot of the white part outside the colored iris, but dogs and cats show little or none. Gorillas have black "whites" to their eyes, whereas owls' eyes are so large that the two nearly touch inside their heads. Humans and dogs have round pupils; cats' pupils are vertical slits; and those of goats and sheep horizontal. All these facts, when correctly depicted, contribute to the convincing effect of a picture.

Ears are more complicated than the triangular flap they often appear to be. The flap is only the top part of the ear, and quite complicated shapes can be seen at the rear of its base, though fortunately perhaps this is sometimes partly hidden by fur. The hair growing inside and around the ear also deserves careful examination, for when it is well understood and drawn, it helps to give a picture the right character. In fact this applies to hair patterns in general — their inclusion adds interest and authenticity to a picture. But they must be understood if they are included, for depicting them inaccurately is worse than leaving them out. This applies to any feature of a painting: omit what you do not want to include, but do not put in something that is not there.

Feet can also be a source of difficulty. It is often difficult to tell how many toes an animal or bird has, particularly as they are frequently half-buried in fur or feathers. It helps to be able to handle the animal, but this is not always advisable or possible. Looking at and drawing museum specimens is also useful for such information, but remember to allow for their rather stiff and shrunken state. With birds' feet, the arrangement of the toes when perching can be obscure — one or two can be seen, but it is not always clear whether all the others are at the back of the foot or merely hidden by feathers. One may feel that if they cannot be seen, it does not matter, but knowledge helps one to draw the parts one can see with greater understanding.

At first sight *a hoof* is not like the conventional foot with four or five toes; it has changed over the millennia to fit the needs of a running animal, whose life depends on its being able to run faster and further than animals with paws, claws, and sharp teeth. However, the hoof begins to make sense when you realize that it is the one remaining toe in horses — or two in cattle, pigs, and other cloven-hoofed animals — with a greatly enlarged and strengthened toe-nail. It keeps a hoofed animal literally "on its toes," ready to run and keep running from danger.

The drawings of some of these features on page 17 are done in a fairly detailed way. This degree of finish will obviously not always be wanted in a picture, but the structure needs to be understood, however impressionistic the rendering of it may be. It is remarkable how a drawing with little specific detail can still manage to convey the complete structure, so long as the artist himself is aware of that structure. There is magic in an apparently random scribble or brushmark by someone who knows and has observed the form, for it implies the whole underlying structure without apparently defining it at all.

Fur, feathers and hair

(*see also page 18*)

The texture of fur, hair, and plumage can be conveyed in many different ways in watercolor. The different treatments employed will depend on the character of the paper, the speed with which the picture is to be done, and the scale of the picture as a whole and of the animal within the picture.

The example on page 18 show possible ways of conveying long and short, fluffy, shaggy, and smooth hair and feathers. There are other ways to do it, some of which will be seen in the illustrations throughout this book. But, however one is working, one point to keep in mind is that the shinier the subject, the greater the difference in tone between the darkest and the lightest parts, and the more sharply they are divided — a shiny surface reflects light, and on those parts where no light is reflected, the tone is very dark. Similarly, the finer the size of the individual hairs, the less they can be seen as separate objects; so that fine hairs may be shown either as the smallest of brushmarks or left out, although it is permissible to put in a few to indicate hair growth.

To show the fluffy or woolly character of fur or down, the paper may be wet with clean water and the wash allowed to spread to give a soft, indefinite edge. If a coarse woolly or shaggy look is needed, whole locks of hair can be done in this way — the cloudier the look required, the more general the application of color.

A velvety texture to some extent combines the characteristics of a smooth, shiny surface and a fine, fluffy one. It seems logical, therefore, to portray it through a considerable difference between its darkest and lightest tones, but with no sharp change from one to the other, as with a smooth all-over wash, darkening in tone fairly suddenly, but very smoothly.

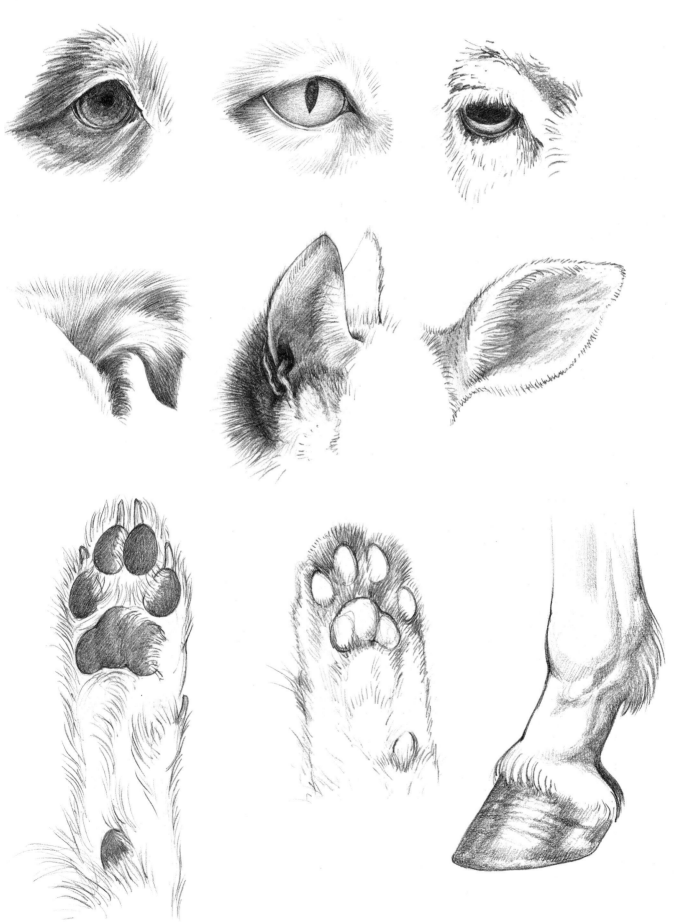

ANIMALS
AT REST

Animals at rest

The first demonstration on pages 22 – 23 is of a sleeping cat. The cat has a habit of adopting many unconventional positions in sleep — at first on her side, curled up, but after a time stretching, rolling over, and settling for the next period of slumber into a posture of uninhibited relaxation. Many pencil drawings were done in preparation and the drawings reproduced are only half the number done. Several were sufficiently complete to serve as a basis for a finished picture. Some of the incomplete ones were left unfinished because the cat moved; others were drawn as detailed notes to clarify the structure or position of feet or ears.

Of the complete figures, I chose for my picture one that shows the cat in an unexpected attitude.

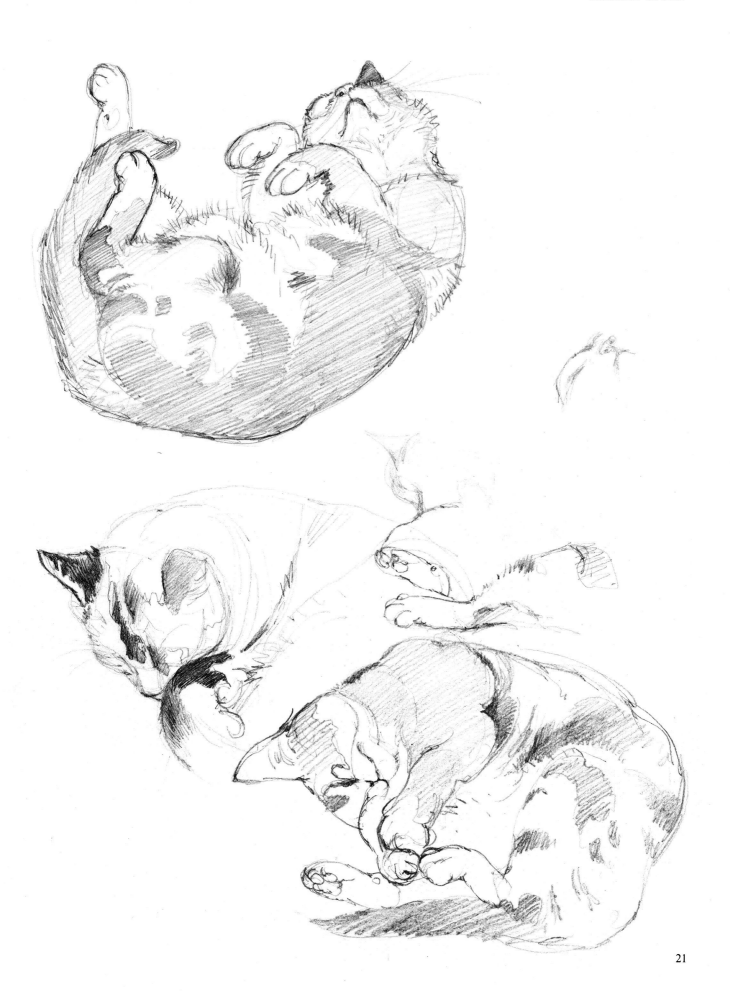

Stage 1

Sleeping cat: demonstration

Original size: 8¾ in. sq. (225 mm sq.)
Paper: Mold-made Fabriano 140 1b. (300 gsm)

The first stage of any picture is, strictly speaking, looking at the subject and choosing which aspect of it to work on. This stage has been discussed on page 20, so we will call stage 1 of the demonstration that point at which the business of putting the chosen composition on paper begins.

Stage 1

Choose a suitable paper and redraw the cat carefully in the required size, with the tortoiseshell markings lightly indicated and the folds of the rumpled candlewick bedspread carefully drawn. This stage is very important and must not be hurried. If possible, compare your drawings with the cat itself, as well as with your original sketch. The cat will not be in the same position, but its component parts will not have changed, and you will be able to check on such details as number of toes and the relative position of ear, eyes, and nose. Turn your picture upside down and look at it in a mirror. Often this will reveal slight errors of drawing, and these must be rectified now — if you let them pass, they will haunt you later.

Stage 2

This is a simpler stage. I first go over the whole background with clean water, not quite up to the edges

Stage 2

Stage 3

of the cat. A thin mixture of cobalt blue and Payne's gray is then washed quickly over the damp paper with a large brush. Next, with a fine brush, the wet color is carefully taken up to the edges of the cat.

When this is dry, the main color of the cat (burnt sienna and yellow ocher) is put all over those parts of the cat which are not white, building up the blotches with stronger color before it is dry. The toes, nose, and ears are added with a thin mixture of permanent rose and cadmium red light.

Stage 4 — Finished painting

Stage 3

A similar method is used to add the cat's black markings with a wash of lamp black. The color must be floated on very delicately so as not to disturb the color beneath. I use a thin, wet wash, adding a stronger mixture of pigment and water as it dries to give the range from solid black to mixed black and ginger stripes. A very weak wash of yellow ocher and black is used to model the white area, and the folds in the cloth are defined with a strong blue-gray mixture, weakened where required with water.

Stage 4 — Finished painting

Apart from the addition of a few details of hair, whiskers, lips, nostrils, and variations of the color of fur with patches of yellow or burnt sienna, the main work of this stage is the candlewick texture of the blue cloth. This takes a long time, but it justifies the effort by enriching the picture. The lines of blue-gray, dark or pale according to their place on the folds, help to define the shapes and form an interesting contrast to the irregular pattern of the cat's markings.

23

Capturing your subject

The drawings on these two pages are of animals not actually asleep but in resting positions. There will always be some movement, but unless your subject actually walks away, it is possible to continue drawing the body and working on the legs and head when they are in the right position. The best approach to your subject is probably to draw the whole figure as quickly as is consistent with a careful look to sum up the elements of the pose, and then to continue, for as long as your model remains, to develop the drawing, correcting if necessary and filling it out with more detail and more thorough development of the forms.

The three pictures here are all made with different media, although in each, watercolor is used to a greater or lesser extent. The white dog is a pen drawing with a small amount of watercolor — the pen line suits the subject, whose outstanding characteristic is the coat of longish, disordered curls: the fine line indicates the shape of these without falsifying the light tone. The cat has more watercolor in its composition — in fact the entire ginger part of its tortoiseshell pattern. The black part, however, is done with a thick soft pencil, as is the main figure.

The other dog is painted almost entirely in watercolor, but soft white chalk has been used on the long, plumy hair of its tail and ruff. This mixture of media is very useful in depicting animals. So often the character rests on the convincing rendition of a rather diffuse, but quite definite, pale or white texture or pattern of fur over a much darker background — this is a method that can be used successfully for this purpose.

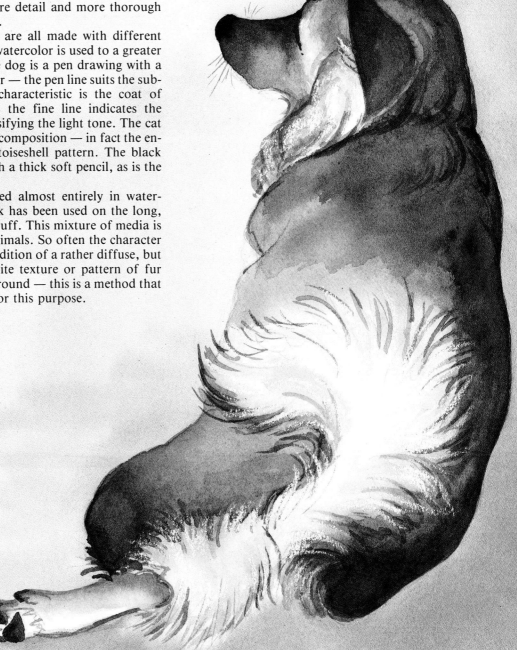

Stage 1

Stage 2

Sitting dog: demonstration

Original size: 11½ × 8¾ in. (290 × 222 mm)
Paper: Handmade 200 1b. (410 gsm)

Stage 1

This lively young dog does not stay long in any one place. The pose is chosen from preliminary sketches in varying degrees of completeness, and a pencil drawing then made on a rough handmade paper.

I wet the background well with clean water, up to about ¼ in. from the edges of the animal. As she is mostly white, the background is used as a simple contrast, to define the figure. While the water soaks into the paper, I mix a plentiful supply of color: manganese blue, phthalocyanine blue, and yellow ocher. I wet the paper again, then as quickly as possible apply the color to the background. With a smaller brush, I take the color up to the edges of the dog while the background is still wet, thus allowing the texture of the paper to give some variety of tone and color to this background wash. The edges are softened in places with a clean, wet brush, but these areas must be allowed to dry completely before any more work is done.

Stage 2

The color for the patches on the dog's face is mixed with yellow ocher and burnt sienna and washed on. The tone is built up by applying more color as it dries to model the form of the face and ears.

Stage 3 — Finished painting

The golden yellow eyes, brownish-gray nose, collar, and name tag are added. When they are dry, the nostrils, pupils, and the edges of the eyelids and lips are defined. The white parts of the dog are now given a little more modeling with a pale mixture of yellow ocher and black. In this picture the pencil drawing plays an important part, being used to indicate the hair and details of feet and muzzle.

Stage 3 — Finished painting

These pencil sketches demonstrate the preparatory work that goes into the finished painting, although only the dog (left) was drawn with a definite outcome in mind. This was one of many studies made of a pair of Norwegian buhunds (a dog like a small elkhound) and forms the basis of the watercolor on page 25. The tiger cubs and caracals (middle right) were drawn on visits to zoos. I make as many of these sketches as time allows, intending to select later on suitable, attractive subjects for paintings.

My cat (bottom) is frequently drawn, both for practice and as the subject for illustrations and paintings.

ANIMALS
IN MOTION

Animals in motion

When animals move, the difficulties of drawing them obviously increase enormously. Also, the faster the movement is, the greater the difficulty of seeing, let alone drawing, the mechanics of the motion. There are several ways in which enlightenment can be sought.

It is possible to perceive certain positions or postures that a moving animal seems to hold for rather longer than others. These are the stages in the whole sequence of positions that will best portray the action, and they are the right ones to pick for your drawing. The great difficulty, however, lies in seeing for certain the relationship to each other of all parts of the animal at a given moment in the course of the action.

The sequence of drawings below, and on page 29, are based on two sequences from a great volume of photographs of moving animals and humans done by Eadweard Muybridge (born Edward Muggeridge). In the latter part of the nineteenth century, he devised a means of photographing moving animals at regular, minute intervals. By this means, he provided an answer to questions that had stumped experts (according to Plato) since the time of the ancient Egyptians. The drawings on page 29 are based on photographs selected from one of Muybridge's sequences of a walking horse; those on this page and the next derive from his photographs illustrating the canter. Many other gaits and animals are shown in his work — cattle, deer, pigs, raccoons, cockatoos, ostriches, pigeons, dogs and cats, as well as horses. The same information is now supplied by cinematograph film and video, which are particularly useful in showing slow motion to the artist.

Constant drawing of moving animals — that is, recording the positions of legs, neck, and tail, rather than attempting any comprehensive representation of form — will not only supply information but develop one's ability to perceive action. Drawings done at this speed must be used only in conjunction with others done at greater leisure or with a study of the animal, referring back to your action sketches. Still photographs of the same species or breed can also be used, so long as one refrains from copying a photo and instead uses the information to augment that obtained from your drawings.

Another valuable aid to understanding the process of movement is some acquaintance with the anatomy of the animal — not necessarily in great detail, but enough to help you understand what underlies its outward appearance: which parts of it are fixed, which parts move and in how many directions; which parts can be stretched and which cannot. This subject is dealt with on pages 96–97, but from the drawings it can be seen that the movement of the fore and rear legs arises in different ways. The hind legs pivot from a point about halfway down the body, where the thighbone articulates with the pelvis; the forelegs' action arises from the top of the body, the shoulder blades moving with the foreleg bones and pivoting from the level of the backbone. This can be seen in the drawings on pages 96–97, which are based on more of Muybridge's photographs, with lines superimposed to show the positions of the leg bones.

While a thorough study of anatomy is not necessary, reference to the workings of the skeleton and muscles can illuminate a puzzling question in drawing an animal. There is much to be said for getting into the habit of referring to the skeleton whenever you find a form difficult to draw. At times it is hard to work out just why a subject is as it is, but this can be clarified by going a little deeper into the matter, until the difficulty lessens and disappears. Many museums have at least some animal skeletons.

After some familiarity with the skeleton has been achieved, it can be very useful to augment this by finding out in a practical way how the skeleton is moved by the actions of a living animal. In the course of stroking and fondling a reasonably even-tempered cat or dog, one can glean a lot of useful information about the positions of bones, the relative lengths of different parts of the skeleton, and the range of movement of the various joints. Gently and slowly moving the legs about can be most illuminating; it is important to study this aspect of an animal's appearance, as well as the static forms.

The drawings on this page all represent endeavors to capture movement in varying degrees: gentle, slight motion of the tail and head in the cow and calf sketch (one of the preparatory studies for the demonstration on pages 118 – 119); rapid turns, bucking, and galloping by the gnus (left). As these were drawn from television, with its constant changes of viewpoint, I had to work even faster than when drawing directly from the living animals.

The raccoon's steady prowling round and round his small enclosure meant that I saw the same view of him at regular intervals, at least until he changed his route. The common toad might seem to present less difficulty in this respect, but he can move with quite a bit of speed.

Run, rabbit

The positions of the rabbit at the bottom of this page — three stages of a fast run — show what a considerable distance is covered by each stride. Both pairs of legs stretch out horizontally; the hind feet overtake the front feet as they touch the ground, and the powerful hind legs give another strong push, which propels the animal far forward. The feet work very nearly as separate pairs, front and back, but they are very slightly out of sync with each other — though so slightly that to the unaided eye it looks as though each pair of feet were moving together.

Other animals move their legs almost simultaneously in pairs, but in a different arrangement — both left legs, then both right legs together. These tend to be large, heavy animals such as bears and elephants, and also old cats and dogs.

In attempting to draw moving animals, it is helpful to spend a considerable time simply watching, as there is no doubt that familiarity with the subject makes drawing it correctly both easier and quicker. In spite of the near impossibility of accurately fixing the sequence of limb movements of a fast-moving animal by the eye alone, as you watch it becomes clear that certain positions are characteristic of a particular action and convey it most clearly. Perhaps this is because these positions are held just a little longer, but whatever the reason, it is so. Studying the photographs of, for instance, all the horses running together in a race will show that the positions of some of the horses look right, conveying swift and energetic movement. Others, however, will look rather odd, almost awkward, though obviously they, too, are moving their legs in the correct order.

It cannot be overemphasized that in drawing a moving animal from life, even the slightest, most incomplete drawings are of value and well worth keeping. Any unfinished detail may prove to be the one that provides the exact piece of information you need, perhaps long afterward, when used in conjunction with other drawings done on different occasions. If all your drawings of a particular animal, or kind of animal, are kept together and referred to when you embark on a painting, so that you have all the data at your disposal, you are giving yourself the best chance of producing a good, sound piece of work.

A moving animal seems almost to change its shape as it moves, not merely its position. A neck that, in repose, seems almost nonexistent can extend in a way that suggests its structure is like that of a telescope. In fact, the truth is more likely to be that the skeleton of the neck is flexed, almost folded into a double curve within its wall of muscles, and hidden in a loose and elastic covering of furry skin, so that when its owner wishes to strike forward suddenly, or to see over an obstruction, the whole extends itself very fast and to a surprising length. Seals and cats are particularly gifted in this respect. Both seem able at will to vary their shape from a very long and slender one to something approaching the spherical. A cat sitting outdoors on a cold day will be very little longer than it is wide; its head will be settled comfortably well into its shoulders, its legs tucked under its body, and its tail wrapped round to keep out the draft. The same cat, reaching up to a tabletop or a door handle, will change those proportions completely, becoming twice its former length and half its width.

The running rabbit shows some of the same kind of change of shape; although the neck is not extended, the body and legs alternate between long and narrow, and bunched up and compact.

Cat up a tree: *A plump domestic cat, which when not exerting itself presents the appearance of comfortable indolence personified, is transformed into an athlete when it climbs a tree. It positively runs up the bare trunk to the branches. Not all cats, however, are equally skillful at coming down again. If the distance is too great to be leapt, some will display rather less confidence on the downward journey, but some — and by no means necessarily the most slender and adventurous ones — will make the descent with as much speed and skill as they showed on the way up.*

Stage 1

Stage 2

Alsatian puppy: demonstration

Original size: 9 in. sq. (225 mm sq.)
Paper: Mold-made Whatman 90 lb. (180 gsm)

This young Alsatian, past the stage of infancy but still a puppy in behavior at about six months of age, does not stay still for long except when asleep. Many quick drawings were made, and several were combined to supply the basis of the chosen pose. One drawing showed the entire body and legs, so that nothing was invented. The position of the head was taken from another drawing, in which the body was incomplete.

Stage 1

The final drawing is done from life, working over a basic redrawing of the first sketches. It is not necessary to see the dog in an identical position — the information was obtained at the first sitting, and now only needs to be developed into a firm pencil study by means of constant reference to the animal.

Stage 2

After the eyes are given their base color of mixed burnt sienna and yellow, the background is wet all over. A mixture of phthalocyanine blue, cadmium yellow light, and Payne's gray gives the desired grayish green and is used to build up a preliminary tone around the form of the dog, although the final tone will be adjusted later.

Stage 3

Stage 3

When the background color is absolutely dry, a ground tone mixed from yellow ocher and burnt sienna is washed over the dog, varying from very pale to a warm brown on the head and other parts, where extra burnt sienna is added to the still-damp wash. The background tone is built up with the gray-green, with extra Payne's gray added to the mixture.

Stage 4 — Finished painting

Stage 4 — Finished painting

A wash of lamp black, varying from thick to very thin, is put over all those parts of the dog where the coat is black or where black hairs lie over the brown. Some ultramarine on the flank gives the light reflected by the glossy black hair. A thin black wash is put on the pads and used for details of the dark hairs; the light hairs are defined with opaque yellowish white. Details on the eyes and muzzle are defined in black, and highlights touched in with opaque white and gray. The final tone of the background can be built up a little more if desired.

Everyday activity

While it is natural to think of an animal in motion as one which is walking, running, leaping, climbing, or in some way proceeding from one place to another, there are many other kinds of movement that can provide interest in a picture. A few are shown here, portrayed in some different ways.

The little dog scratching its ear is drawn with an extra-thick soft pencil; the cat lapping milk is painted with a black wash on wet paper, with a few details added once the wash is dry — eyes, tongue, ears, a few hairs, and the blue saucer.

The cat washing is also done with a single wash, but on a dry surface, so there is not the soft, diffused edge one gets on a wet ground. Much more detail was added over the wash after it dried — the stripes, details of feet, ears, and more hairs, including the hair growth pattern on the back of its neck.

The fourth figure, the sleeping cat, is drawn with a fine brush. Here the hair is defined to a still greater extent. A slight wash of tone was added to the detailed brush drawing, which was then completed with the addition of the pink ears, nose, eyelids, mouth, and toes.

Leaping cat: demonstration *(pages 38 – 39)*

Original size: 11½ × 8¾ in. (290 × 222 mm)
Paper: Saunders 90 lb. (180 gsm)

In order to maintain the impression of fairly rapid movement in the picture of a cat leaping down from a height, I decided to use a generally fluid, loose treatment. The picture is almost entirely in closely related colors in the yellow to red sector. A constrasting note is supplied by the green eyes and black pupils.

Painting animals in watercolor

Stage 1

Stage 2

Stage 1

The cat is drawn as it nears the ground — the front paws in position for landing; the hind feet coming forward and down, ready to hit the ground immediately afterward, the toes spread in preparation. The eyes are put in with pale green.

Stage 2

A wash is put over the entire background — pale, warm yellow at the top, graduating to warm brown at the bottom. A very small amount of violet is added at the bottom left corner so that the background hues are not identical with those of the cat's fur.

Stage 3

The whole cat's body is washed over with diluted burnt sienna, ranging from dark on the back and face to nearly white on the underside of the animal's left foreleg.

Stage 4 — Finished painting

The cat's markings are added with a thicker burnt sienna wash, softened at the edges. A darker color is used to delineate the ears, hair, fur, nose, and forms round the eyes, with black for the pupils.

Stage 3

Stage 4 — Finished painting

Stage 1

Stage 2

Fox: demonstration

Original size: 9 in. sq. (225 mm sq.)
Paper: Mold-made Whatman 90 lb. (180 gsm)

Stage 1

The figure of the fox is carefully drawn, using many studies from life and from filmed wild animals. Details and measurements are checked by referring to photographs and to measured drawings made from dead specimens. This study is then developed into a pen drawing, with the essentials completed but the finishing to be done later.

Stage 2

Pale washes are applied: cobalt blue for the sky; blue-green on the field; yellow ocher and a variety of greens in the foreground, some bright and yellowish, some with more blue.

Stage 3

Stage 3

The same process is taken further, using a blue-gray-green for the bush on the right, yellow-olive for the oak trees in the background, and a brighter green for the other distant trees. A mixture of green, yellow, and brown is used for the fence posts, burnt sienna for the sorrel, yellow ocher for the dried stalks of cow parsley, dots of yellow for the flowers, dark green for the nettles, and a stronger, bluer green for the clumps of reeds. A basic wash of burnt sienna is then put over the figure of the fox.

Stage 4 — Finished painting

Stage 4 — Finished painting

The figure of the fox is now completed with a black wash of varied strength: intense on the feet and muzzle; thin on the body and tail. The texture of the paper enhances this combination of two separate washes.

A great deal of detail is added to the background, both in watercolor (notably the bright yellow-green leaves around the left-hand fence post and foliage) and in pen (details of branches, leaves, grass, reeds, posts, and wire). The same is done for the fox, with whitish hairs added on the the tail, head, neck, chest, and rump, and pen drawing used for details of the hair, toes, claws, eye, and whiskers.

Birds flying

How birds fly can be dealt with here in only the most general terms. Considering the size of most birds and the fact that in many cases their fuel comes in very small units — from insects, seeds, caterpillars, or berries — their ability to fly at all seems incredible. Migratory flights of many hundreds of miles represent quite extraordinary activity for a creature whose weight is often only a matter of ounces.

To lift even so small and light a body as a songbird's, and to move such relatively large appendages as wings, requires muscles that, in relation to the bird's size, are massive and powerful. This in turn requires a large, steady frame for these muscles, proportionately large lungs to sustain the considerable effort of flying, and a streamlining of the head and body so that they can go through the air without providing any more resistance than is necessary. It is these considerations that govern the typical bird shape: more or less oval, with no sudden protuberances, and legs that are usually drawn up like a retractable undercarriage (except for the long legs of storks, flamingoes, and similar birds, which trail behind them).

When drawing, the same considerations apply to fly-ing birds as to galloping horses — observe as much as possible, and study photographs to confirm and expand your observations. At least when birds glide, as do many of the most impressive long-distance fliers, it is possible to see what they are doing as they soar and swoop.

The shape of a bird's wings is governed by its way of life. Vultures, eagles, and albatrosses all fly vast distances or soar to great heights, and remain airborne for long periods. They thus have long wings with strong primary feathers to control their soaring and gliding, and to make the most of wind and rising air.

Geese, swans, and other heavy, large-bodied birds, which also fly great distances in regular migrations, have broad wings both to lift their bulk (with a great deal of noise) and to keep them flying strongly to and from arctic and temperate zones.

Small birds that live among bushes and trees have rather short wings and so can fly safely between the branches.

DOGS

Dogs

Although the domestic dog is a single species, the range of dogs' sizes, shapes, and coats is extraordinary. It shows what can be achieved by interfering with the course of nature and causing animals to breed together in order to intensify particular characteristics — what might be termed "unnatural selection." Theoretically any dog will breed with any other; in practice, of course, enormously exaggerated discrepancies in size can prevent such inter-breeding from being achieved successfully. There is no doubt in the mind of a dog, however, about his close relationship with a bitch of another breed.

The results of "accidental" crosses are as good dogs as their artificially engineered relations, and often as handsome. Indeed, one may feel that in this respect they are superior to some of the dog breeders' flights of fancy.

Dogs who are incapable of breathing normally, like bulldogs; whose backs cannot support their own weight, like dachshunds; whose eyes are easily dislocated, like Pekingese; or who are too small to give birth safely by normal means, like the smaller chihuahuas — these dogs are not the result of matings arranged by the dogs themselves but of those masterminded by man.

The drawings on this page show some of the variations of the build, proportions, and coat of the products of dog breeding.

The top one, an elkhound, is the closest to the wolf-like animal from which all domestic dogs are most probably descended.

Next, a greyhound — one of the oldest of breeds, with long legs and long jaws.

The dachshund is the victim of breeding that has nearly gotten rid of its legs; it suffers greatly from slipped discs.

The King Charles spaniel has an abnormally short nose and an abnormally long and wavy coat.

The fox terrier shows no extraordinary distortions. It was born with a normal tail, but this was cut off.

Anatomy and physique

The drawings on this page show some of what underlies the outward appearance of some dogs; they also demonstrate the extent to which the skeleton's proportions have been altered with selective breeding. The two skeletons shown here started from the same point, but whereas the top one is almost the same as its early forebears, considerable modifications have been made to the skeleton of the other. The short legs mean that the upper leg bones consist of little more than the two ends; the middle part has been reduced to almost nothing. Nevertheless, the relationship between the two is still very clear.

These alterations to the dog's physique were begun with a purpose in mind, of course, and most breeds have a perfectly sensible build and pleasing appearance. It is when these breeds are no longer bred for the original purpose, or when the standards are set only for competing in shows, that the desired physical characteristics become extreme and appearance takes on more importance than performance. When modern specimens of a particular breed are compared with photographs of dogs of that breed from a century ago, considerable differences are seen — short legs are shorter, pushed-back noses have been pushed back almost in line with the eyes, long coats have become a floor-length curtain of hair. Where the dog has continued to be used for its purpose, there has been a divergence between the working and show types, as with collies. Working collies have continued without much change during this century; the present-day rough-coated collies have a larger nose and longer, silkier fur, though they still retain their shepherding instinct. Some may even occasionally work with sheep.

The lower drawings show the differences between a normal dog's skull and the greatly distorted one of a bulldog. Here again, the change began for a purpose: so that the dog could grip a lump of bull with its teeth without its nostrils being stopped up. At the beginning of the century, the nostrils were about halfway between the front teeth and the eyes; now, when very few bulldogs need to have their noses anywhere but in the front of their faces, they are about as far back as they will go, and bulldogs have to snuffle and gasp for breath.

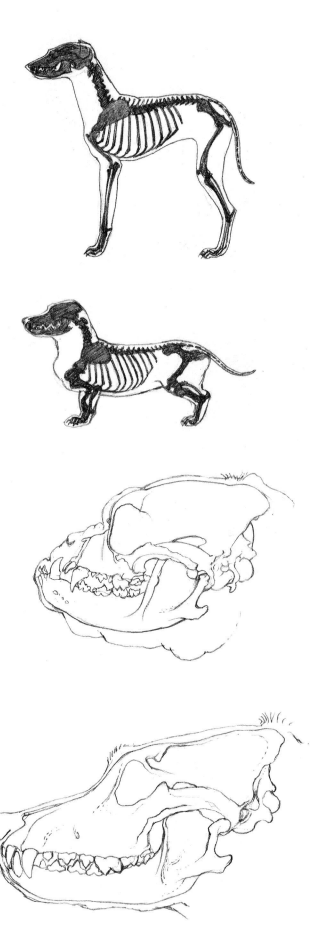

Dog walking: demonstration

Original size: 7¼ × 15 in. (185 × 375 mm)
Paper: Saunders 90 lb. (180 gsm)

The gait of a dog walking on its own is quite different from that of a dog on a lead. The golden labrador in this picture ambles along, sampling the interesting scents left by previous travelers.

Stage 1

As always, the drawing is of prime importance. It is not essential to include a lot of detail as long as you have detailed studies to work from, or the living animal. It is vital, however, that what you draw is in the right place.

Stage 2

The background is left vague, with simple washes of color to suggest a rough path and greenery. These washes are applied to previously wet paper in bands of yellow-green, with darker, bluer green above and grayish brown below.

Stage 3

When everything is thoroughly dry, a light wash of yellow ocher is put all over the dog — much paler on the inside of the far hind leg and on the lower parts of the face and neck; deepened and warmed up with burnt sienna on the crown, ear, neck, shoulders, rump, and tail.

Stage 4 — Finished painting

All the sharp detail is added now. A black wash, with some burnt sienna, is used to model the structure of the face, mouth, eye, and nose. These are built up with a less watery mixture, until finally it is almost full strength, to give the head considerable prominence. Further washes of warm brown are used on the ear, neck, shoulders, and tail, where darker hair overlies the pale coat. Fine brushmarks indicate the lie of the hair and point up the details of the ear, eye, and paws.

Stage 1

Stage 4 — Finished painting

Stage 2

Stage 3

The Spitz group

These dogs are the nearest in appearance to wolves — although not necessarily in size, as they range from the Eskimo dogs, which are like wolves and have in fact been known to interbreed with them, to the toy pomeranian. The characteristics of the group include upright, pointed ears; tightly curled tails; pointed noses; and a thick, springy coat.

The breed illustrated is a samoyed. Other members of the group are elkhounds, chows, keeshonds, and buhunds, a dog like a small elkhound. The purposes for which these breeds were used are many — huskies for hauling, chows for food, elkhounds for hunting, pomeranians as lapdogs, spitzes for watchdogs as well as for hunting, buhunds for cattle herding, keeshonds for keeping on barges (presumably as watchdogs).

The samoyed picture is almost in monochrome: the only patch of color is the pink tongue. Apart from the eyes, nose, and mouth, the drawing consists mostly of hair — the coat is very dense and weather-resistant.

Spaniels

The spaniels and their related breeds have been bred mainly for retrieving and are capable of carrying things in their mouths without inflicting damage. They also tend to plunge into water whenever the opportunity arises. There are many breeds of spaniel — the cockers (British and American); springer, clumber, and water spaniels; King Charles spaniels and papillons. Setters are in effect tall spaniels; retrievers and labradors may be regarded as related breeds.

Spaniels have silky, often wavy or curly coats; long, soft ears, rather domed heads; and soft, baggy mouths. These drawings are studies of various spaniels. The color illustration is of an English cocker spaniel; here again, much of the work consists of putting in the hair, which is much softer and smoother than the samoyed's, and wavy.

Mastiffs

Mastiffs are one of the oldest breeds of dog — a dog very similar to our present-day mastiff is shown in Assyrian reliefs. Most large, heavily built dogs can be classified as varieties of mastiff: St. Bernards, Pyrenean and Bernese mountain dogs, Great Danes, and New-foundlands. Bulldogs and boxers might also be included in this group.

The mastiff in the picture, unlike the previous two animals, is short-coated, so that its powerful, heavy build is clearly seen. The skin on its head is looser and hangs heavily round its lower jaw and above its eyes. The picture required careful drawing, but the water-color treatment is straightforward and direct, with sim-ple washes over the drawing and a little reinforcement of details with a fine brush.

Terriers

The terriers form a very large group, varied in build and ranging in size from Airedales as big as retrievers, down to Yorkshire terriers, minute but well able to speak up for themselves. By definition, terrriers were bred for digging out unfortunate animals that had taken refuge underground. They come in almost any color: black and tan (Airedales, Manchester and Welsh terriers); black (Scottish terriers); blue-gray (Kerry Blues); white (West Highland terriers); tawny (Cairns); red-brown (Border terriers); yellow (Irish terriers) or white with patches of tan, black, or brown (fox terriers and Jack Russells). Legs vary from long (in Airedales), to almost nonexistent (in Sealyhams).

The picture is of a wire-haired fox terrier — much the same animal as the smooth fox terrier on page 44 but with a wiry, springy, weather-proof coat. Comparison between the two pictures illustrates how, when drawing a long-haired dog, one must remain aware that what lies under the hair is an animal with muscles, bones, and tendons.

Although at a cursory glance such an animal may look shapeless and the arrangement of hair disordered, the position of each lock of hair is determined by its place on the solid dog beneath. Thorough study of the animal reveals this, and careful drawing will show both the nature of the coat and the form of the dog inside it.

Old English sheepdog: demonstration *(pages 52 – 53)*

Original size: 11½ × 8¾ in. (290 × 222 mm)
Paper: Saunders 140 lb. (300 gsm)

The shaggy coat and general build of this dog make it a suitable subject for a very free, quick treatment. Inside the long, thick coat is a large, normally shaped dog, but the waving locks of hair are what fill the view.

Stage 1

First draw the figure of the dog on an absorbent, medium-rough paper. The gray parts of the dog — its ear, back, and haunch — are then given a freely brushed wash of slightly bluish gray.

The whole shape of the dog is then outlined with curly brushstrokes of masking fluid. This process is continued over all the parts of the dog I want to keep white or very pale.

Stage 2

A very pale yellow-gray is used on some of the parts in the light, as they need a little tone to show the individual

Stage 1

Stage 2

locks of white fur. So more masking fluid is added to protect this color, and another medium-gray wash is then put on to the shadowed parts of the dog's face, head and body.

Stage 3

I make sure that the dog's shape is protected by masking fluid sufficiently far in from its edges to permit me to brush on the background color with considerable speed. I then prepare two mixtures of color: one of manganese blue and a little Payne's gray; the other of Winsor violet, Payne's gray, and a little ultramarine.

These are applied in bold, free strokes, diagonally, in a way that lets both colors be seen and also lets them mix. In places, I drag them over the paper, and I let a little of it remain uncovered.

Stage 4 — Finished painting

It is essential that the work be allowed to dry thoroughly before the solidified masking fluid is rubbed off; otherwise, it may damage the surface of the paper. When this is done, the dog is revealed, standing out cleanly against the background. A very dark bluish gray is used for some more shaggy locks on the gray parts of the body and ear, and the black end of the nose is added. This treatment gives the pleasing appearance of a print.

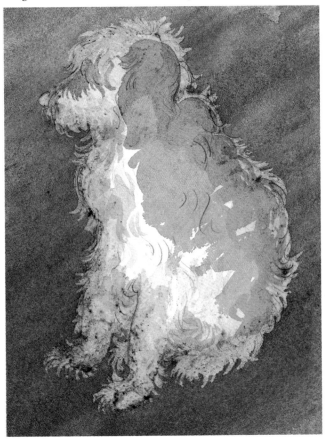

Stage 3

Stage 4 Finished painting

Greyhounds

Greyhounds are another very ancient group, bred for coursing — running down hunted animals, however swift — and they are capable of considerable speeds. Our own racing greyhounds show clearly the shape of the dogs. Salukis, Afghan hounds, borzois, Irish wolfhounds, and Scottish deerhounds are very like them under their hair, and whippets and Italian greyhounds are smaller versions of the same animal.

They are well-proportioned, graceful dogs, strong and deep-chested — essential to accommodate large, powerful lungs.

The member of the group illustrated below is a Saluki, the Persian greyhound, said to be scarcely changed in 5000 years. This dog is a pale, creamy color, smooth and shiny, with long, wavy hair on the ears and tail, and fringes on the legs and feet. A smooth, thin wash is used for the body, with the form indicated in deeper tones. A thin black wash defines the muzzle and details of the face, eye, and nose. Wavy brushmarks then create the long locks of hair on ears and tail.

Hounds

One tends to count as one group a number of dogs that are used in packs to hunt their quarry by scent: bloodhounds, foxhounds, harriers, beagles, bassethounds, and others. They are used for hunting foxes, hares, otters, and anything else that will run far enough. Bloodhounds were originally used for hunting deer and were brought over to England by William of Normandy. They are used for finding people now, of course, and have the ability to follow a scent as much as four days old. This kind of fact reveals how a dog's sensitivity to smells is completely different from ours.

The most complicated part of this picture is the bloodhound's face with its folds of skin. Apart from this it is a matter of an all-over wash of light yellowish brown, with black washed over it after it is dry and a stronger mixture of brown used to define the modeling of the legs, feet, and body.

Golden retrievers

Original size: 14¼ × 21¼ in. (358 × 530 mm)
Paper: Saunders 140 lb. (300 gsm)

These two large dogs are golden retrievers — half-brothers, though not particularly alike in face or color. The best arrangement seemed to be one dog sitting upright and the other lying down, both looking in the same direction. This L-shaped composition filled out the space sufficiently without overwhelming it.

A feature of this breed is the long, glossy, brightly colored coat, very thick and red-gold in color.

Many studies are made of the two dogs, in any attitude they happen to assume as I draw. I do this because it is essential to become familiar with their appearance as individuals as well as examples of the breed. The result is a number of pages of drawings of both details and complete figures, some in postures fairly close to what I require for the picture, some quite dif-

ferent. I have studies of paws, hair patterns, facial features, and other details. From all this material I then work out the composition of my picture, drawing on all the information contained in the studies and on memory. I then refer again to the dogs to check the accuracy of my work, and to give authenticity to my portrait of the pair. It will be seen that the individual characters of both are clearly differentiated. The differences are not great, but careful study of the animals while one works on the finished picture reveals the differences quite clearly. Washes of pale golden brown are put over the figures, varied with additions of more burnt sienna in places to give a range of color and tone that shows the glossy texture. Details of the fur are added before the washes are fully dry.

A rather yellowish green is used for the grass on which the dogs are lying, to keep the whole rather light in tone; it is also keeping with the yellow-brown of the

dogs. The green is darkened with burnt sienna and black where it edges the dogs' bodies, partly to add contrast, but also to give weight at the bottom of the the picture.

Stage 1

Stage 2

Pug: demonstration

Original size: 9 in. sq. (225 mm sq.)
Paper: Saunders 140 lb. (300 gsm)

Stage 1

This painting has a simple wash background, as I do not want to distract attention from the complications of the folds of skin on the dog's head and shoulders. These must be carefully drawn before one starts to put on the color.

Stage 2

The background is wet with clean water, and the color applied — mixture of blues: manganese, cobalt, and ultramarine. I keep this light around the head, but make it darker where it adjoins the lighter-toned body.

Stage 3

Stage 3

A very pale wash of yellow ocher is put over the whole dog; some stronger yellow ocher is added along its back and on its tail.

Stage 4 — Finished painting

Stage 4 — Finished painting

A thin wash of black over the yellow ocher gives some modeling to the body, legs, and rolls of loose skin around the shoulders and neck. This wash is built up in stages to a full-strength black, to define the folds on the face and the black mask and ears, as well as the eyes, in which a little burnt sienna and black has been used for the irises.

Opaque white mixed with a little yellow ocher and black is used to define the fur on face, chest, and ab-domen. A light opaque gray then defines the details of nose and mouth, and the folds around the eyes. A touch of almost pure white outside the irises helps to enhance the characteristically worried expression.

Domestic breeds

Complete classification of domestic dogs into groups is impossible; there are so many breeds whose ancestry is not known, and others whose forebears have come from more than one group, as in the case of the bull terrier, a mixture of bulldog and terrier (probably the Old English white terrier). Often, when it is thought desirable to modify some feature in a breed, the change is brought about by introducing a strain of another breed that displays the desired characteristic. For example, the pointer was originally a rather slow, heavy dog; with the development of rapid-firing guns it became desirable to have a fast-mover, so some foxhound blood was bred into the breed.

Poodles are a breed that is not easy to classify with certainty. Originating in Germany, they were used for sheep herding and for retrieving waterfowl, and came to be used for this purpose over much of Europe — so

their function was much the same as a water spaniel's.

The practice of clipping poodles' coats into patterns began as a means of reducing interference with their movements in water and keeping them warm when they emerged. Since those more practical times, man has given full scope to his taste for hair styling and devised many fanciful variations on the theme; two are shown in the picture: a standard and a miniature poodle. The larger, black one's waves and curls are put in over a soft wash of medium black, softened at the edges, with many fine brushstrokes in black and then, using opaque white, in pale gray. The little dog has his curls in similar strokes, but all in a color slightly deeper in tone than his ground color. As always with a long-haired dog, when I work on the preliminary drawing, I draw the inner dog first, and build the thickness of the hair over this.

Mongrels

Although most of the dog pictures so far have been of recognized breeds, one or two mongrels have been included. The parentage of the dog on pages 14 – 15, as well as pages 26 – 27, is unknown, though it seems likely that there is either a large element of Border collie or that mixtures of many breeds have led to a similar appearance. The small white and gray-black dog at the top of page 24 is a cross between a smooth Jack Russell terrier and a white miniature poodle; the little dog scratching its ear on page 36 is another from the same litter, not particularly like her brother. The origins of the dog on this page remain a mystery.

The posture in this picture was chosen from a number of sketches made from life. A basic wash of burnt sienna and yellow ocher was worked into it before drying, with a deeper color used to represent its rough coat and structure on the head and legs. Once this was dry the nose, eyes, collar, and name tag were added.

Stage 1

Stage 2

Stage 3

Detail of the finished painting

Running greyhound: demonstration

Original size: 6½ × 9 in. (160 × 225 mm)
Paper: Mold-made Whatman 140 lb. (300 gsm)

Stage 1

This is another subject where careful drawing must be the first consideration. A pencil outline is used, and the background is kept very simple.

Photographic reference has been used to ensure accuracy. The tongue is colored with a thin wash of cadmium scarlet, and the eye with yellow ocher.

Stage 2

The background of pale yellow-green, mixed from phthalocyanine blue and cadmium lemon, is floated on to the previously wet paper. Stronger green, with a little Payne's gray added, is put into the wet wash below the figure of the dog.

A very weak wash of yellow ocher, with a little burnt sienna, is put over the face, the inside of the far legs, the belly, the front of the near thigh, and the dog's right hind foot.

Stage 3

At this stage the main color of the dog's coat is added, using a stronger wash of yellow ocher, and blending this color where it ends with the very pale parts already established, so that there are no hard edges between the dark and pale parts.

Detail

This detail of the greyhound painting shows how bones, tendons, and even blood vessels show through the thin, close coat of the animal, just as they do in a thoroughbred horse. This has been conveyed by the application of darker, more sharply edged patches of tone than those used for the broader forms on which these details lie.

Stage 4 — Finished painting

Stage 4 — Finished painting

The final building up of deep tones is done at this stage with successive washes of almost pure burnt sienna and of black on the muzzle, neck, chest, thigh, and feet. The muscles and veins are defined, and even stronger black used for the pupil, mouth, nose, whiskers, and claws. Details of the ears, eye, and feet are strengthened, and the pencil line built up in places with a black wash line.

Painting animals in watercolor

In making studies, it is often necessary to concentrate on the overall posture and proportions of the animal, rather than on the detailed structure of noses, ears, and eyes. Separate small drawings are then made to show the exact construction of these features, and it is interesting to compare the variations in the different breeds. The drawings below compare the eagerness of development of the folded skin around the jaws of the buhund, a dog like a small elkhound (top), spaniel (middle, right), and mastiff (bottom, right); the widely differing ears of the buhund and of the spaniel and bassethound (bottom, center) with the greater length and weight of their upper part; and the varied looseness of the folded skin around the eyes of the bassethound, St. Bernard, and bloodhound (all bottom, left).

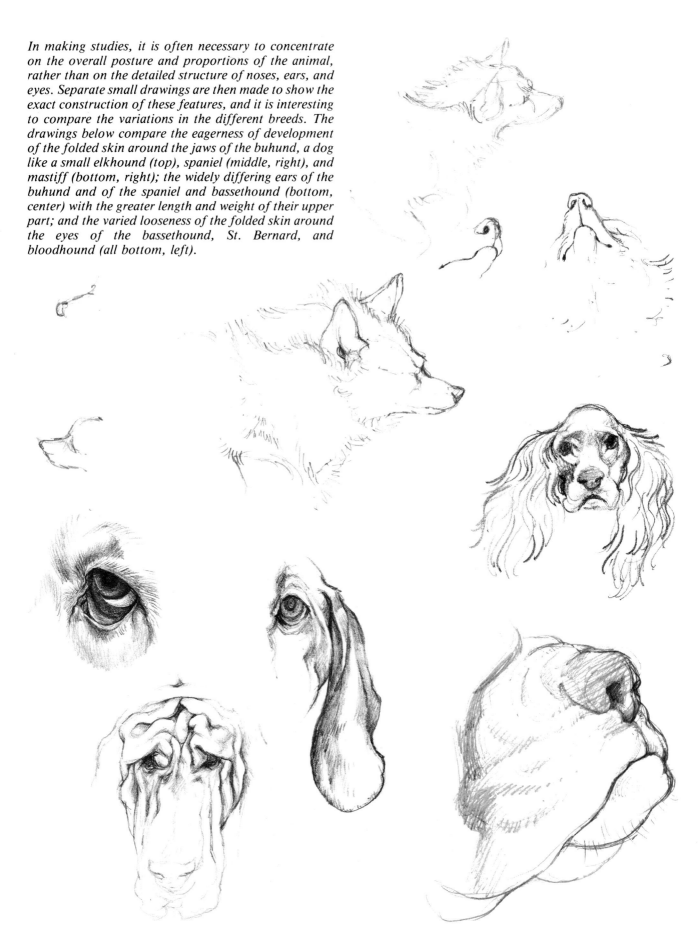

Stage 1

Stage 2

Stage 3

Stage 4

Dog, digging: demonstration

Original size: 7 × 8⅝ in. (180 × 220 mm)
Paper: Saunders 90 lb. (180 gsm)

This picture again uses masking solution but to a lesser extent than in the Old English sheepdog painting.

I use it to define the edges of the animal, so that a wash can be put freely over the background, leaving a clean edge. This process lets the brown and white dog stand out against the green and sandy-colored setting; at the same time it helps to define the character of the subject's coat. The short, rough coat seems best conveyed by using fine brushmarks, in brown and gray, on the

pale yellow-brown and white patches of hair. On the other hand, using opaque white, I provide a contrast in tone, with pale yellowish and white brushstrokes on the dark and middle-toned areas.

Stage 1

The dog (that most dedicated digger, a Jack Russell terrier) is drawn carefully and the features of the background lightly indicated. With all these pictures, the animals have been very carefully drawn beforehand, often more than once, and the final result carefully traced so that the drawing can be reproduced without harming the delicate surface of the paper.

I then apply the masking fluid all round the edges of the animal, with indications of hairs where these interrupt the outline, as on the head, neck, tail, and elbow.

Stage 5 — Finished painting

Stage 2

The daisies in the grass are then stopped out, and all this work with masking fluid is then allowed to dry thoroughly before I embark on the painting of the background. The far background is painted into wet paper – a pale lemon wash with a hint of phthalocyanine blue, above it a dull green obtained by adding Payne's gray. While this dries, space can be left for the patch of grass behind the dog, and a ground of yellow ochre with burnt umber washed across at the level of the dog's feet.

Stages 3 and 4

A deeper yellow-green (cadmium lemon, phthalocyanine blue, and burnt sienna) is blobbed on for the overhanging foliage in the top right-hand corner. Slightly watered down, it is also used for the two grassy areas. The detail of the grass is added with a darker mixture, and little variations of color are made with touches of yellow and extra blue in the mixture.

When the background is absolutely dry, the masking fluid is removed from the edge of the dog's shape. A yellow ocher and burnt sienna wash, stronger than the brown-yellow ground, is put on to the dog's patches, inside the hole, and around his feet for the lumps of soil.

Stage 5 — Finished painting

I now add the black and gray detail of the eye, nose, ears, and paws, and quite a lot of elaborate work on the outline of the animal, defining the growth of hair and the smoother forms of the legs. Some paler gray is used to indicate shapes on the head, body, and leg, and at this stage I add the brushmarks defining the hair.

The masking fluid is now removed from the background, leaving the daisies sharply defined in the grass. Yellow centers are added. A few blades of grass are allowed to grow up in front of some of them.

CATS

Cats

Cats are perhaps the best subject for an aspiring animal painter to start on. Even if you do not have one of your own, other people's cats seem to spend many hours contemplating the world from garden walls, doorsteps, and pavements. Often they are friendly and approachable enough to permit stroking and head rubbing, which will help you to increase your knowledge of their structure.

If you have a cat of your own, it probably spends plenty of time sleeping, and this will present you with an ideal subject on which to practice.

Whereas dogs vary enormously in size and shape, cats are very much alike in these respects — there is variation, but within much narrower limits than with dogs. There is considerable variety of color and pattern, however, some of which is shown on these two pages. The plain colors include black, white, brown, beige, and blue-gray. The patterns include blotched, striped, and spotted tabbies; every possible variation of random patches of black and white; pale with dark face, tail, and legs; patches of tabby on white, and variations of color of the tabby pattern, from gray and brown through a large range of orange, red, yellow, and apricot. More complicated still is the tortoiseshell, where there are random patches of white, black, and red tabby, which can be in either the blotched or the striped tabby pattern. These may be mixed in any proportion, and can be very muddled and hard to sort out, but it is not safe to make up a tortoiseshell pattern unless you thoroughly understand the underlying principle.

The illustrations show a black and white cat with a fairly common arrangement of the two colors, a ginger (red tabby), a blue (this one is a Blue Persian, but the color occurs in short-haired cats as well), a white, and a tortoiseshell. There are of course many others; I have picked out only a few examples to illustrate some of the color varieties.

The differences in conformation among domestic cats are dealt with later in this chapter, but it may be interesting to consider how consistent the conformation

of all the wild cats is. Apart from extreme differences in size, with tigers at one end of the scale and the little black-footed cat at the other (slightly smaller than the average domestic cat), the shape of the whole family of Felidae is extremely consistent; some have shorter legs than others, or wider heads, or shorter faces, but the differences are less than in many other families. Lions and tigers look very different, partly because of the difference in color and pattern, and particularly because of the presence of the mane and tail tuft in lions. Under their skins, however, lions and tigers are indistinguishable, though I believe that the largest tigers (the Siberian ones) can reach a size greater than lions. This may be because the biggest tigers are those found furthest north, while the lion's range is greatly restricted, particularly in its northern reach. Perhaps all the really large lions have become extinct; tigers in the extreme south of their range are considerably smaller than their northern relations.

Stage 1

Stage 2

Tabby cat: demonstration

Original size: 9 in. sq. (225 mm sq.)
Paper: Saunders cold-pressed 140 lb. (300 gsm)

The cat chosen for this demonstation, a striped silver tabby, is strikingly marked, so I decided to present a straightforward side view and provide a contrast in color by means of a simple wash background.

Stage 1

The drawing is quite a complicated one in that the pattern of the cat's coat is the main feature of the composition and must be drawn accurately. As these patterns obey certain rules, although showing variations, it is desirable for the markings to be clearly indicated at this stage in order to be finished correctly later.

Stage 2

The background is wet thoroughly with clean water, nearly up to the edges of the cat, but not quite reaching them. This is in order to prevent the water, and later the background color, from spreading over the edges. Then the wash of yellow (cadmium light) is put onto the wet background, but again not right up to the edge of it (so that there is no risk of a dry edge where you do not want it). It is finished with a finer brush and the color taken carefully up to the outline of the animal. While the yellow background is still damp, a mixture of cadmium

Stage 3

red light and burnt sienna is dropped into it where the orange is required. The yellow of the eye and the pink nose and ears can also be put in at this stage.

Stage 3

When all the work done so far is absolutely dry, a very pale gray wash is applied over the figure of the cat, and this in turn is allowed to dry thoroughly.

Stage 4 — Finished painting

Stage 4 — Finished painting

The markings of the cat's coat are now added with a strong lamp black wash; this process should be made simpler by all the work and care spent on the drawing. The edges of the markings should be softened where pale fur merges into black. The picture is finished with such details as the fur, the pupil of the eye, and whiskers.

Cat conformation

Although the differences in build between one type of cat and another are not very great, there are nevertheless three distinct types into which cat breeders divide them.

Longhairs: This group includes the so-called Persians, angoras, chinchillas, and similar cats. Longhairs are of fairly solid build, with short legs and short noses, and of course, long hair. They come in all colors. The illustration (above) is of a black longhair.

British shorthairs: These have a round head, thick neck, deep chest, and strong legs, longer than those of the longhairs, but not excessively so. Again, most colors are represented. The picture (left) is of a British blue shorthair.

Other shorthairs: This group includes the distinctive Siamese, Abyssinisian, Russian Blue, and Burmese. These cats have long heads, narrowing to the nose, large upstanding ears, thin legs, long thin tails, and a close, short coat. The one illustrated (right) is a Siamese.

Most ordinary house cats come somewhere in the middle of these. The average cat's shape is compact, adaptable, yet athletic when it needs to be.

Tabby patterns

There are two distinct kinds of tabby pattern: striped and blotched. They are quite different from each other and never appear together on the same coat. The striped tabby pattern — which may vary in the length of the stripes, so that some cats have stripes broken up into short pieces that could be described as spots rather than stripes — is very close to the patterns of some of the wild cats. I once had a cat which was almost identical in markings to the Kaffir cat, *Felis Lybica,* which will interbreed with domestic cats. These markings have considerable beauty and provide wonderful camouflage. My striped tabby, sitting under shrubs on a sunny day, was practically invisible from four feet away.

The blotched tabby pattern (page 75) has no counterpart in the wild, and is presumably a mutation of the striped tabby pattern. It is a difficult pattern to draw as, although it seems to be random, it is virtually impossible to make up convincingly. It is always worth taking the trouble to draw it carefully from an actual cat.

Siamese cat: demonstration (pages 76 – 77)

Original size: 11½ × 8¾ in. (290 × 222 mm)
Paper: Mold-made Whatman 200 lb. (410 gsm)

Stage 1

The cat is drawn in the allotted space and needs fairly careful placing, since the figure spans almost the whole depth of the picture and comes very close to its edges.

Stage 2

The whole background is wet with clean water and given blue washes — pale above (a weak mixture of manganese blue and cobalt blue) and dark below (a mixture of phthalocyanine blue, ultramarine, and a little black), where it will set off the pale body of the animal. These blues have been mixed to tone with the billiant blue of the cat's eyes, which are filled in with a strong, bright mixture of cobalt and manganese blues. When this is almost dry, a drop of clean water is dripped into the middle and mopped out with a squeezed-out brush — this gives depth and transparency to the eyes.

Painting animals in watercolor

Stage 1

Stage 2

Stage 3

A pale wash (a very little yellow ocher and phthalocyanine blue, and a little black) is put over the whole cat. A wash of black with a little yellow ocher is put over the legs, tail, ears, and face, washed out to merge into the light parts. A stronger yellow ocher and black wash than the pale ground color is used to strengthen the fur color on the chest, throat, and legs.

Stage 4 — Finished painting

A fine brush and near-black are used to define the eyes, mouth, nose, and ears, and for the vertical pupils.

Opaque white is mixed with a very small amount of yellow ocher and black and used extensively to brush in fine hairs on the head and body, ears and whiskers. It is used in a darker mixture on the legs and for drawing toes.

Stage 3

Stage 4 — Finished painting

Kittens

New kittens show considerable differences in proportion from adult cats. If attention is not paid to these differences and their exact nature, it is difficult to draw kittens convincingly. It is difficult anyway, since they move so quickly and so suddenly.

I have made some drawings of kittens' heads and of complete kittens that may shed some light on their characteristics and the way they develop from newborn infant to adolescent. It is surprising what a difference paying attention to these details makes — for example, having whiskers of the right length immediately establishes that you are drawing a kitten of a particular age.

The newborn kitten, of course, has its eyes shut, and they stay shut until about ten days after birth. Usually they begin to open at the inner corner and have a rather oriental look until they open completely. They are, like a human baby's eyes, a smoky blue, and change color gradually to yellow, green, amber, or clear blue. When the kitten is first born, its ears are very tiny and far down at the sides of its head; the flap of the ear is not yet present. As the kitten grows, so do its ears, which appear to move up its head, although this apparent movement is really more a matter of the different size of the upper part of the ear in proportion to the lower part.

The whiskers are short and very fine at birth, of course, and they grow and coarsen as the fur grows. The fur itself is sparse in a new kitten, which appears quite bald on its underside, muzzle, and feet, though in fact the tiny soft hairs are present and quickly grow to an attractive coat of fluff. By the time a kitten is starting to leave the mother for brief periods of play, the fur on the tail has grown sufficiently to give it the shape of a young fir tree — wide at the root and pointed at the tip.

The nose and muzzle of a very new kitten appear proportionately large, which is not unreasonable considering the importance of the mouth and its use. There are no teeth, of course. As the face develops and the fur and ears grow, the characteristic cuteness of large, bright, forward-looking eyes; large ears; and small, delicately formed nose and mouth appears.

The body of the kitten shows similar changes. Newborn kittens have rather frog-like little legs, too weak to lift their bodies off the ground. They appear to be almost swimming as they move, and they spend a certain amount of time lying on their backs, waving their legs slowly and helplessly until they manage to get the right way up. They grow quickly, however, and within a few days of opening their eyes they are staggering, with legs spread wide and stomachs just off the floor. Before long, they can find their way to that part of the house where the food is kept. They very quickly begin to vary their diet from one of only their mother's milk. I once had a kitten that at five weeks or so would climb to the highest vantage point it could reach and scream for hand-outs of cheddar cheese.

Often kittens are extremely active and adventurous before their mother is ready to let them go, and she will spend hours following her errant brood and carrying them one by one back to the box. Each time she sets out for another kitten, she is overtaken by the one she has just deposited, on its way back to join its brothers and sisters. By this stage the kittens have changed completely from their infant state; they have become longer in the leg and their feet seem disproportionately large. By six months or so they will have reached adult size, though they are not yet as solid in the body or as serious in temperament as they will be in maturity.

Capturing kittens at play

It is a pity to draw kittens only when they are asleep or suckling, but as they move so quickly when they are playing they are a very difficult subject to catch. All the rules about drawing moving animals apply, but the postures assumed by kittens at play can be very surprising and change rapidly. In addition, more than one animal needs to be drawn, as they are most often playing in a group, jumping on each other and rolling over together. This makes it an advantage to use a piece of conté crayon or a wash brush — or any medium that produces a fuller mark than an ordinary pencil or drawing pen — so that one can depict the whole body and head instead of one edge of it. These drawings can be used in conjunction with the more detailed, measured drawings one can do from the sleeping animal. Reference can also be made to photographs; these are particularly useful for checking proportions of one part of the animal compared to others. These considerations are important for, if a mistake is made, the effect of the age of the kitten can be missed. If the head is too small, for example, it will look too old.

Most drawings you do of kittens at play will probably be unfinished, but they will be lively in a way that more carefully worked-out drawings rarely achieve; they are done in response to your direct and immediate reaction to what you see and can form the basis of more considered work later on. It is not easy to do, but if you draw active subjects whenever the opportunity occurs, it will become progressively simpler.

Stage 1

Stage 2

White cat on a colorful ground: demonstration

Original size: 9 in. sq. (225 mm sq.)
Paper: Saunders cold-pressed 140 lb. (300 gsm)

The purpose of this picture is to demonstrate how an interesting and colorful painting can be made by concentrating one's efforts almost entirely on the background — after the drawing stage, that is. It does not mean that time and attention are not spent on the drawing. On the contrary, the edges are so important in such a composition that, if anything, they need extra care.

Stage 1
Quite a long time is spent on this part of the picture, as it is important that the perspective of the patchwork squares be correct.

Stage 2
The cat is more or less completed at this stage, apart from the individual hairs that go over its outline. A pale pink is put on the nose and the edges of the ears, and a very pale yellow-gray is used to indicate the modeling of the head, paws, and tail. The same color, but a little darker, is used for defining details.

Stage 3

Stage 3
This stage, the most striking phase of the picture, is simple to describe, but lengthy in execution. Each square in turn is washed with color, and by blotting color or flooding in stronger pigment where required, the folds and rumples of the cloth are depicted. All the squares are green, blue, or purple, but great care has to be taken to maintain variety in these colors so that the background is clearly a piece of genuine patchwork, not a mechanically repeated pattern.

Stage 4 — Finished painting

Stage 4 — Finished painting

Small details complete the picture: hairs on the edges of
the cat (done with opaque white and a no. 0 sable
brush), whiskers, and tiny stitches on the seams of the
patchwork.

This theme lends itself to many interesting variation. I
have given it the same kind of treatment in pastel, where
the subject was a black animal and the picture done on
black paper, defined with a brightly colored background.
A patterned rug or richly colored embroidery could be
substituted for the patchwork.

Cat with kittens

Original size: 6¾ × 9¼ in. (170 × 230 mm)
Paper: Mold-made Saunders 90 lb. (180 gsm)

A cat with a litter of small kittens makes an appealing picture. The subject has the advantage of being reasonably static, yet the small movements of the kittens' paws massaging the mother as they suckle prevent it from being too immobile. It can present some difficulty in drawing, as the kittens lie on top of or burrow underneath each other, and sometimes look like a mass of fur with a number of assorted, disconnected legs. Careful observation with intelligent analysis of what you see is the important factor in drawing. Understanding is all; the marks you put down on paper will follow with comparative ease.

OTHER DOMESTIC
ANIMALS AND
BIRDS

Other domestic animals and birds

Apart from dogs and cats, the animals that live in our homes include creatures of many sorts, such as guinea pigs, hamsters, mice, gerbils, and rabbits; canaries, parakeets, parrots, and myna birds; fish and turtles.

There are many species of small mouse-like animals, and many of them look alike. Obviously there are differences, but these are often minor and are only discovered in the course of the close examination that is so essential to any drawing. The speed and suddenness of their movements, however, can make such study difficult. The structure of their minute feet, the placing and direction of their often surprisingly long whiskers, the rich texture of their thick and colorful fur, and the size and shape of their ears all need to be examined thoroughly. Getting these things right is what will make your picture of an animal an unmistakable portrayal of an individual of a particular species.

These small creatures can be very timid and nervous, and they should only be handled if they are accustomed to it. When drawing these, or in fact any animals, be particularly careful about the eyes. So often what is otherwise quite a reasonable drawing is spoiled because the eyes have been made too big, giving an unpleasant appearance of artificiality and "cuteness."

The mouse (below right) has settled into an almost spherical shape. This particular mouse is a common wild one, while the ones usually kept as pets are differently colored varieties of the house mouse. Hamsters (below left), have become very popular in the last few years. The gerbils (opposite) are a more recent enthusiasm, though the guinea pig (below) is a domestic pet of long standing.

Compare the handling of the paint in the guinea pig and hamster pictures, where two completely contrasting kinds of fur are shown. The wavy brushstrokes show the long, wavy hair of the guinea pig. In contrast, with the hamster the areas of wash, darkening at the edges of the forms but with little intervening delineation of texture, depict the quite different, almost velvety character of its fur.

The method used for all of these studies is similar — careful drawing at first, a wash of the ground color of the subject, successive washes of color to build up gradations of tone, some modeling of the form, and an indication of hair patterns and detailed features at the end. The treatment of these subjects is freer than many of the paintings earlier in the book.

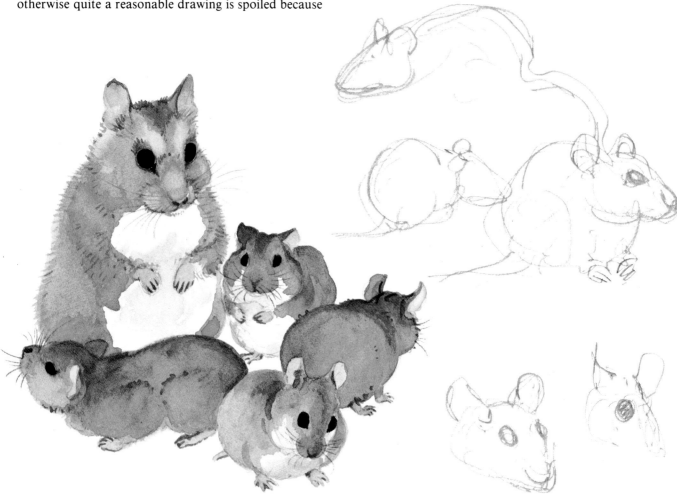

Stage 1

Stage 2

Parakeet: demonstration

Original size: 9 in. sq. (225 mm sq.)
Paper: Mold-made Saunders 140 lb. (300 gsm)

This is another painting with a complicated composition, which has to be carefully worked out. The bird perches before an all-over pattern of leaves and a lattice of stems.

Stage 1

The drawing is carefully transferred to the paper, and a strong wash of yellow (cadmium lemon warmed up with a little cadmium yellow) is put on the whole bird except for the eye, beak, blue patch, feet, and tip of the tail.

Stage 2

The branch, twigs, and leaves are painted in pale washes: weak burnt sienna with a little yellow for the twigs; a grayish blue-green (yellow, Payne's gray, and a touch of phthalocyanine blue) for the leaves; a slightly brownish gray for the branch.

Stage 3

Stage 3

A thin wash of brilliant blue-green (phthalocyanine green) is mixed for the bird's body and laid on very lightly over the yellow to allow it to show through the green. Take care, however, not to lift it and cause it to become mixed with the green. The beak and eye are now put in with a medium gray and black.

Stage 4 — Finished painting

Stage 4 — Finished painting

The black markings on the head, neck, wings, and tail, as well as the details of texture on the branch, are now added.

A strong wash of manganese blue is put on to the tail, with its fullest intensity at the tip and merging into the green where the tail meets the body.

Tropical fish

Original size: 14¼ × 21¼ in. (358 × 530 mm)
Paper: Mold-made Whatman 140 lb. (300 gsm)

This painting of an aquarium with tropical fish is an
ambitious one, and one that cannot be hurried. The
lighting of the tank means that the background is varied
in tone. Some of the weeds are lit up brilliantly, while
the thick growth throws other parts of the interior of the
tank into deep shadow.

Care must be taken that the picture does not become
so confused that the subjects (the fish) get lost among
the variously lit elements of their setting. The fish,
which are shiny and iridescent and usually brightly colored as well, are on the whole shown up best by a dark
background. But if the entire interior of the tank is
darkened, there is no source of light to account for the
illumination of the fish. Also, such a large area of dark
background would make a less interesting picture. The
way out of the difficulty seems to be to place most of the
fish so that they have a background that enables them to
show up, although we can afford to have a few that are
not well lit in the interests of realism.

The individual fish are interestingly varied in shape
and color: some are brilliant, some strikingly patterned,
some very delicately colored, with markings that look
faint at one moment and lit up with color at the next.
The scales of all the fish are of a silvery iridescence that
comes and goes with each fish's movements.

Cockatoo

Original size: 12¼ × 8¾ in. (305 × 220 mm)
Paper: Mold-made Whatman 140 lb. (300 gsm)

The sulphur-crested cockatoo lacks the brilliant color of
so many of the birds of this family — parrots, macaws,
and cockatoos being among the most colorful of birds.
Yet, with its pure whiteness, the soft texture in its white
feathers, and its magnificent, striking pale yellow crest,
it does not suffer by comparison. These birds also have
the reputation of being some of the best talkers.

The painting is done quite simply. The background of
grayish green is put on previously wet paper, with
yellow used for the raised crest feathers. The same color
is applied on wet paper to the cheek and underside of
the tail feathers. Very pale gray indicates the edges of
the white feathers; darker gray and black, the claws,
beak, and eye; while gray-brown is used for the perch.

HORSES

Drawing horses

The drawings on these two pages are characteristic of those which an animal painter is constantly making in the course of his work. When, as in this case, the purpose is to study how animals move, the number of separate drawings is greater than when one is working on a less mobile subject, and the degree of finish is deliberately not high. The drawings shown were done from a television broadcast of show jumping. They had to be done very quickly, in short bursts, for the television presentation constantly changes its viewpoint — how often one longs for another second's view of a horse! But television is a great blessing, bringing into one's home so many sights that one might never otherwise see, and sometimes in the sort of closeup that would never be possible.

Only one of these drawings includes the rider, as the main purpose was to record the action of the horses.

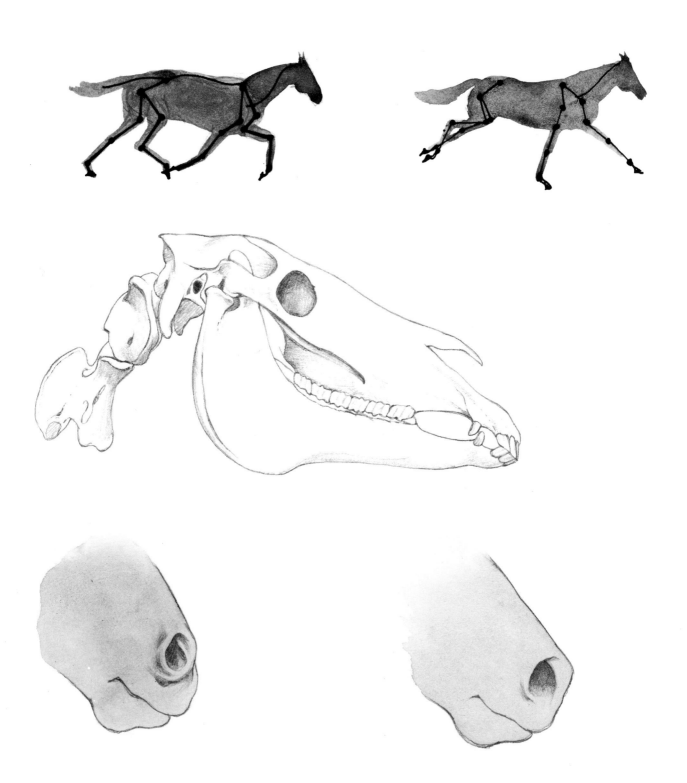

Anatomy of the horse

When you are drawing horses, a knowledge of their anatomy is of great assistance. For instance, when you draw a horse's head, it is remarkably easy to place the eye too low — with all hoofed animals, the eye is rather high. In general, their heads have a large amount of face to a small amount of brain.

The drawing of the horse's skull (middle) shows the position of the eye very high up. The two drawings opposite demonstrate how the ear pivots and will sometimes appear to be forward and sometimes right behind the head.

The small figures of running horses, with lines showing how the legs articulate, illustrate another important point — namely, the position of the forelegs and the considerable distance between the leading leg and the

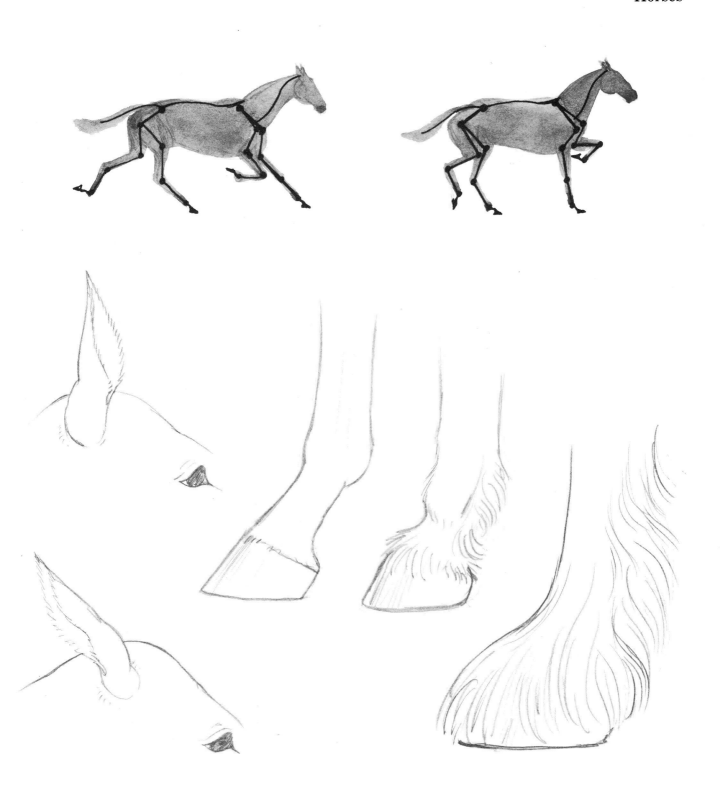

trailing one, which are widely separated where they emerge below the chest. The lines show how the forelegs pivot from a point at the top of the body. They also show that the bones of the leg itself move as one unit with the shoulder blade and that it is at the upper end of this bone that the movement originates.

The drawings in the bottom left-hand corner show a horse's nostril in repose and how it is greatly extended when the horse is exerting itself and breathing deeply. This completely changes, of course, the shape of the animal's face, the end of the muzzle becoming almost square. This change must be taken into account when you are drawing a running or jumping horse.

The three drawings of hooves compare the feet of different kinds of horse. First, there is the long, slender, sloping pastern of the thoroughbred, built for speed. It can be compared with the conformation of the feet of such dogs as greyhounds. Second is the shorter, more upright shape of the cob; and, third, the huge, hairy foot of the shire horse.

Stage 1

Stage 2

Work horse: demonstration

Original size: 6¼ × 9 in. (160 × 225 mm)
Paper: Mold-made Whatman 140 lb. (300 gsm)

The work horses — the shire, Clydesdale, Suffolk Punch, and Percheron — have a special charm. Impressive in their massive strength and size, and endearingly gentle and good-tempered, they suffered from a drastic reduction in their numbers with the mechanization of farming. These horses were also used by breweries, and in England some of the surviving large breweries have retained their work horses and contributed to the revival of interest in them.

Stage 3

Stage 1

After a careful drawing of the horse is made, the background is dealt with before continuing on the animal. Some pale blue (cobalt) and gray clouds about the horizon (cobalt with a little burnt sienna) are washed in, in very light tones. The field is also washed in, very pale, with yellow-green (lemon yellow, phthalocyanine blue, and a touch of burnt sienna) and pale yellow ocher, in irregular zones of color. For the nearer trees, some yellow-green, a little bluer than the grass, is used.

Stage 2

The distant trees (an even bluer green) and the rough grass of the field (more burnt sienna in the green) are added at this stage, as well as the fence on the far side of the horse's field.

Stage 3

Now the nearer trees are finished with quite a dark brownish green, slightly blued here and there. They are darkest where they appear behind the fence on the right.

Stage 4 — Finished painting

Stage 4 — Finished painting

The horse now has its dappled pattern added, with a gray mixed from Payne's gray and burnt umber, put on so as to leave white spots. Darker gray spots are dabbed on as the wash dries. Detail is added to sharpen the eye, nose, ears, mane, and tail, and the edges are strengthened. The hooves are finished in gray and yellow ocher.

Horse's head: demonstration

Original size: 9 in. sq. (225 mm sq.)
Paper: Mold-made Whatman 90 lb (180 gsm)

I have chosen a direct profile view of the head of a thoroughbred for this demonstration. I have also used a method rather different from the other ones in this book: doing an underpainting in monochrome, with the color put on in a separate operation.

As usual, the preliminary step is an extremely careful drawing. When the horse is the subject of a painting, it easily attracts criticism because of horse lovers' tendency to find imperfections in the picture rather than in the model. So when you embark on your picture, you must decide whether you want to paint an idealization of the breed or the portrait of an individual animal. My own taste is for the portrait, "warts and all," but the alternative is perfectly acceptable. To achieve it, one must study many different animals regarded as possessing the required qualities. Photographs are of great use here, as measurements can be made and one compared with another. When you do this, take care to allow for distortions of dimensions due to the position of the camera in relation to the model; look carefully and assess whether it was level, high or low, from behind or in front, or an absolute profile. Knowledge of anatomy is useful here, to analyze the information photographs convey.

Stage 1

Stage 1

The drawing is transferred to the chosen paper; then, with a wash of a brown mixed from burnt umber and ultramarine, a careful monochrome underpainting of the form is built up. This tone is applied only where it is necessary to darken the overall color — the light parts are left untouched.

Stage 2

The background color is put on, and the tone varied by darkening the ultramarine and Payne's gray wash with additional gray.

Stage 2

Stage 3 — Finished painting

Stage 3 — Finished painting

The whole is now left to dry thoroughly — this is where a hairdryer can be very useful. But do not start using it too soon, or you may get unwanted hard edges. However, it can be very useful when the paper is generally damp without any actual wet patches.

The color of the horse's hair is mixed (in this case, burnt sienna with a little yellow ocher) in a fairly thin wash and applied quickly over the whole head. When this is dry, the eye, mane, and the sharp details around the nostril and mouth, as well as odd hairs, are added with a stronger black. A little opaque white is used to mix a gray to highlight the mane.

Shire horse

The pictures of the shire horse on this page and the thoroughbred mare with her foal opposite show how these two types of horse differ. The shire, which sometimes weighs as much as a ton, has the legs necessary to support this weight, as well as an enormously strong physique. It can pull a weight of five tons and is probably the descendant of the great horses that used to carry knights-in-armor.

The painting is carried out in a very sketchy, washy style, with details kept to a minimum.

Thoroughbred

The thoroughbred, of course, is bred for speed, with long legs, a slender build, and a refined appearance. The huge industry that has been built up around it — flat racing, breeding, and training, let alone betting — involves vast amounts of money and people, yet it all started with three horses: the Darley Arabian, the Godolphin Arabian, and the Byerley Turk.

The picture is executed with a fairly free, washy technique. The animals have been drawn with a brush line in black. The grassy background is little more than a plain wash of yellow-green, with tufts of grass drawn in dark green with a no. 1 brush, except where dark green has been washed over the ground beneath the mare; here the grass is drawn in a very pale opaque green.

The glossy, smooth coats are painted with free, broadbrush strokes in varying tones of brown, with strong and weak black washes for the manes, tails, noses, and legs.

Stage 1

Stage 2

Horse looking over a fence: demonstration

Original size: 11½ × 8¾ in. (290 × 222 mm)
Paper: Mold-made Whatman 90 lb. (180 gsm)

Stage 1

The first stage is a pen drawing of the horse; the position and size of the animal have been previously roughed out on the Whatman paper used for the painting, and the pen drawing is done directly from life. Washes are applied: Payne's gray to the sky, and pale yellow-green to the field in the foreground. A little burnt sienna is added to the green for the embankment, and gray for the distant hill; a darker blue-gray green is used for the distant trees. Yellow ocher and a lemon-yellow-green mixture are added to the horse's field.

Stage 2

Patches of yellow, orange, and sharp lemon are put on the trees in the middle distance, Winsor violet and burnt sienna on the ploughed field, and dark green on the small trees on the left. The fence posts are put in with a green, brown, and gray mixture, and some darker blue-green is added around the horse's feet. A pale wash of pink is put on the nose, then a wash of burnt sienna over the body, leaving the white blaze untouched and blending with the tone on the nose. More burnt sienna is used for the dead weeds in the field.

Stage 3 — Finished painting

The horse is completed with black on the nose, tail, mane, and feet. Ultramarine blue and Payne's gray are mixed for the bridle. Dark green detail in the grass in the foreground and in the piece of hedge on the left completes the picture.

Stage 3 — Finished painting

Horses in a pasture

Original size: 14¼ × 21¼ in. (358 × 530 mm)
Paper: Mold-made Saunders cold-pressed 140 lb. (300 gsm).

This scene is a kind still often seen in the countryside — a peaceful scene of a number of assorted horses and ponies in a large field, with a background of trees and farm buildings. The picture, which is painted with a fairly free, loose treatment, features the varied greens of early summer. Masking solution has been used for the fence, the white horse, and the blossoms.

Donkeys

Original size: 8 × 8½ in. (200 × 210 mm)
Paper: Mold-made Saunders 90 lb. (180 gsm)

These two young donkeys seemed to be seeking the company of human visitors, since they spent most of their time at the side of the field where a footpath ran. I had plenty of time, therefore, to make this drawing of them. They are fairly dark in color, but donkeys often are much lighter, with longer, shaggier coats.

The color used was a mixture of burnt sienna, lamp black, and Winsor violet, washed over the whole bodies, with the tone varied by thinning the color or adding more pigment.

A very light yellow-green is used as a basic wash for the grass, and the clumps of grass are indicated with a darker, olive green, mixed from cadmium lemon and black. Finally, the dark details are added, and a few light hairs on the noses and ears are put on with opaque white with a little purple-gray mixed in.

ANIMALS IN GARDENS, PARKS, AND FIELDS

Animals in gardens, parks and fields

Apart from portraying the animals that we live with, there are many other ways of increasing the scope of one's animal work and interests.

People who live in large cities, particularly those in apartments, may find it impractical to keep pets of their own, but parks supply some contact with or at least sight of animals. Deer can be found in state parks and may even appear unexpectedly in the suburbs. Even a bison like the one shown here can be seen in some parts of the American West — in national parks or on private ranches.

All the parks are full of small birds, and most have gray squirrels. These are often exceedingly tame and will take food from the hands of visitors. This is of enormous help to the eager artist, who can take advantage of the activities of other people, or himself bribe the squirrels to stay and be drawn.

Apart from these opportunities, if you come across animals by the roadside which have been killed by traf-fic but not too badly damaged, these can be invaluable, as through them you can discover the exact structure of feet, ears, fur growth patterns, and other details, and make measured drawings. Draw the head, or limbs, from different viewpoints, and use these studies in conjunction with your drawings from the living animal. They will help you to make a really well-observed and thoroughly worked-out painting. Some drawings of these kinds are shown here; and some of this type of material was used for the gray squirrel demonstration painting on pages 112 – 113.

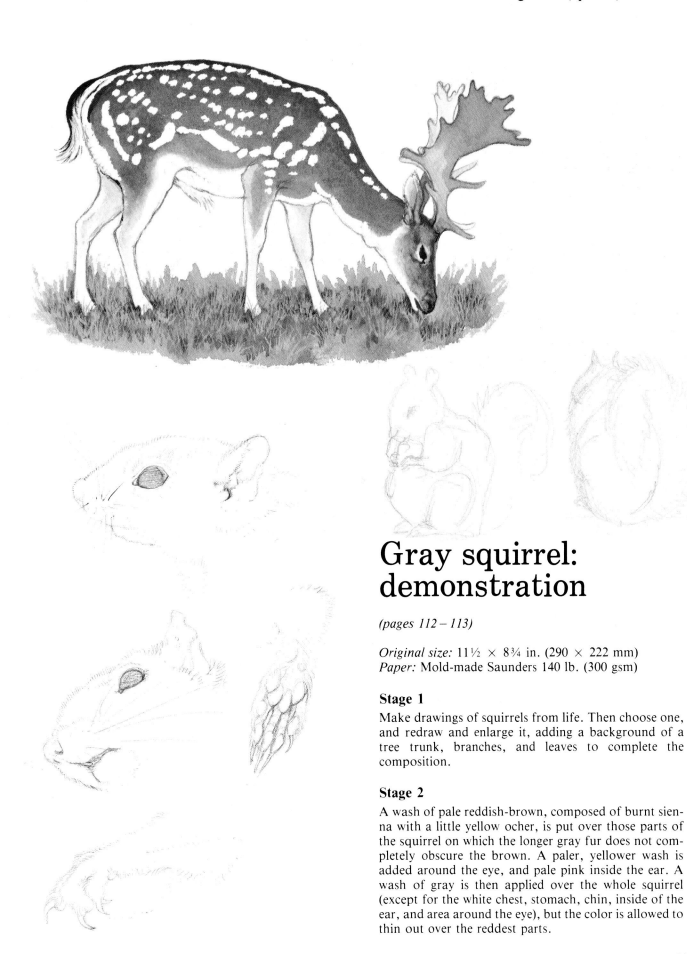

Gray squirrel: demonstration

(pages 112 – 113)

Original size: 11½ × 8¾ in. (290 × 222 mm)
Paper: Mold-made Saunders 140 lb. (300 gsm)

Stage 1

Make drawings of squirrels from life. Then choose one, and redraw and enlarge it, adding a background of a tree trunk, branches, and leaves to complete the composition.

Stage 2

A wash of pale reddish-brown, composed of burnt sienna with a little yellow ocher, is put over those parts of the squirrel on which the longer gray fur does not completely obscure the brown. A paler, yellower wash is added around the eye, and pale pink inside the ear. A wash of gray is then applied over the whole squirrel (except for the white chest, stomach, chin, inside of the ear, and area around the eye), but the color is allowed to thin out over the reddest parts.

111

Painting animals in watercolor

Stage 1

Stage 2

Stage 3

A very pale cobalt blue wash is put on the sky, yellow-green on the trees in the background, and deeper green on the leaves above the squirrel. These washes of green should not be flat, but should have variations in color and tone — yellowish and blue deep tones are used to give variety and form without going into much detail.

A dark brown wash is applied over the trunk and limbs of the tree — a mixture of burnt sienna, black, and a little violet. When this wash is half-dry, a very strong mixture of the same color is used to define the texture of the bark and the edges of the leaves at the top. The squirrel's eye is added in black; just before it is dry, water is dropped into the middle and blotted with a squeezed-out brush.

Stage 4 — Finished painting

The ears, toes, claws, and nose are next defined with a fine brush and many hairs added: long ones on the tail; first black and very dark gray over the central part; then white ones, mainly around the edges, with a few over the central part. The long white hairs form a diffuse outer zone all over the tail, but the reddish color shows through, and also through the similar layer of black hairs underlying the white.

Short hairs are put in on the squirrel's body, head, and feet. The whiskers finish the painting.

Stage 3

Stage 4 — Finished painting

the zoo you can also study foreign animals like the wallaby shown here (a small marsupial related to the kangaroo).

Wild visitors and animals in zoos

Among those wild animals that inhabit gardens, or visit them, are not only squirrels but also many other mammals. In England, for example, hedgehogs will regularly come to the door if milk or food is put there; foxes have moved into suburbs to glean what they can from wasteful humans; badgers, who have always been very shy of people, nevertheless go at night into gardens near their home territories, and in some places they too will come for handouts from the houses' occupants.

Less spectacular, and to many less welcome, are the mice, rabbits, moles, and rats, who naturally think it perfectly safe to settle in for the winter under some flower pot, bucket, or basket that has been left undisturbed for months. Toads are great settlers into compost heaps. One must be careful when jabbing a rake into piles of leaves, since these creatures take on the color of their background.

Apart from these native creatures, there are many wild animals in different parts of the country. Animals like bears, however, are probably best observed in a zoo (or from the safety of your car in a national park). At

The animals illustrated here have been portrayed in varying ways. The *hedgehogs* are painted with a wash of yellow ocher, Payne's gray, and burnt sienna for the head, feet, and lower part of the body; the spines are put in with individual brushstrokes, varying the color to convey the mixture of gray-brown and white on each spine.

The *fox cub* is given a pale red-brown wet wash, largely burnt sienna, with black washed over on the paws, face, and ear. This is done in part while the first wash is still damp and built up further as it dries. The hair, eyes, nose, and edges of some parts are then drawn in with a fine brush using whatever color is called for, from black to light brown. Both of these paintings are done on a fairly smooth cold-pressed Saunders paper.

A much heavier, mold-made Whatman rough paper has been used for the *raccoon* and the *wallaby* — you can see this in the greater degree of texture in the wash. The raccoon is handled similarly to the fox cub, with the addition of opaque white hairs applied over a darker wash.

The *wallaby* and its baby — a *joey* — are painted almost entirely with a wet wash, with burnt sienna mixed with yellow ocher, and thin lamp black washed into the wet ground where required. The brown on the toes of the hind feet, the eyes and inside of the ears, and the noses and whiskers are added after the wash is dry. But the fine details are kept to an absolute minimum, and the character of the paper is allowed to play a major part in the picture.

Working collies

Original size: 14¼ × 21¼ in. 358 × 530 mm)
Paper: Mold-made Whatman 140lb (300 gsm)

This scene of Border collies working with a shepherd to control the movements of a flock of sheep demonstrates the extra interest animals can give to a landscape picture. The setting is a typical hill landscape in the north of England or the southern uplands of Scotland. I did the preparatory work for it in several different ways: drawing dogs and sheep directly from life, drawing sheepdogs working with sheep from British television broadcasts, and taking the landscape setting from drawings done in the past in such terrain, with details of vegetation painted direct from nature. By these means a landscape setting for the central theme was composed to fit the allotted space. This was painted, but the part of the picture where the sheep and dogs were to appear was left unpainted. These were then drawn in lightly, so that when another television program on sheepdogs came up, I was able to make the final drawing of all the figures in effect from life, though of necessity very quickly. A great deal of the preliminary work had been done, although only two dogs were used from the dozen sheets I had previously filled with sketches and drawings of sheep, dogs, and shepherds.

The animals were then finished, and the foreground of grass, the dried spikes of dock plants, the marguerites and poppies completed to round off the composition.

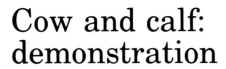

Stage 1

Stage 2

Cow and calf: demonstration

Original size: 9 in. sq. (225 mm sq.)
Paper: Mold-made Whatman 90 lb. (180 gsm)

Unlike most of the other pictures in this book, the cow and its calf are painted in a combination of pen drawing and watercolor.

Stage 1

For the drawing I use a fairly coarse (0.6 mm) technical pen with waterproof black ink — which is, of course, necessary when it is combined with watercolor. On mold-made Whatman rough paper, even this rather coarse pen makes a variable, not very thick, even slightly broken line, although where a solid line is needed it can be achieved by working slowly.

Heavier drawing is reserved for the animals, but the line is kept light in the background.

Stage 2

The foundation of the background is laid in pale washes: very pale cobalt blue for the sky; cadmium yellow merging with yellow ocher for the cornfield; and pale green, with a tinge of yellow ocher at the far edge, for the foreground field, getting deeper and bluer where it reaches the animals' level. To mix the green I use a mixture of phthalocyanine blue, cadmium yellow, and a little burnt sienna.

Stage 3

Stage 3

The trees beyond the cornfield are washed in, with varying greens, mixed from the same pigments in different proportions; the bank of nettles between the two fields is done in the same way. A pale yellow-gray (yellow ocher and black in a very weak mixture) is used for definition on the white parts of the cattle; the same, a little deeper, is used for the hooves. The eyes, noses, and the inside of the calf's ear are also done at this stage, and the light brown fence posts, too.

Stage 4 — Finished painting

Stage 4 — Finished painting

The colored parts of the calf are added in a strong wash of burnt sienna, varying the tone to define the form. The black parts of the cow are painted next in the same fashion. By the time this is done, the calf is dry enough to put in some extra, deeper-toned, detail on the grass around it, in a green with rather more burnt sienna in it. Some softer-edged lines of grass are then added on the further part of the field, with a slightly thinner wash of the same green.

Goats grazing

Original size: 11½ × 20 in. (290 × 500 mm)
Paper: Mold-made Whatman 140 lb. (300 gsm)

For the sake of the color balance of this scene of goats grazing it was fortunate that the nannies were Toggenburgs and that the thistles they were eating at the time were in bloom. This lent itself to a pleasant, gentle color scheme of soft greens, pale purple, and purple brown. The picture shows that a composition can be satisfactorily carried out with only a restricted range of color.

The goats were drawn as they fed, and I made many separate studies. It was necessary to follow them around and through the thistles, as they moved constantly and disappeared among the taller thistles as I worked. From the resulting sheaf of drawings, enough goats were selected to make up a balanced group and were drawn in position. The thistles are, if anything, slightly underdone; they were thick and abundant enough in reality to obscure the goats, so I was rather selective when it came to composing the picture, preferring the main theme to be the goats rather than their food.

I used a fairly free treatment, painting one goat at a time, with a purplish brown mixed from Winsor violet and burnt sienna. First I wet the paper around them, in order to apply a rather misty patch of pale green, alternating with darker green to convey the rough character of the ground around the two animals on the left of the picture. The pale purplish thistles (Winsor violet with a little permanent rose) were added where I felt the composition demanded that color. The diagonal patch from the top right corner forms a link between the separate groups of goats, connecting the small one at the back on the right with the two at the left of the picture, going right down to the left foreground, and then sweeping to the right and enclosing the two nearest animals. The clump of flowers on the extreme left balances its

counterpart at the right-hand side of the picture. When this was established, I completed the thistles with a darker, bluer green for the foliage and strengthened the darker parts of the grass to give weight around the two large goats in the right foreground.

Waterfowl on a lake

Original size: 14¼ × 21¼ in. (358 × 530 mm)
Paper: Mold-made Whatman 140 lb. (300 gsm)

This painting of different kinds of waterfowl on a lake is the result of bringing together several separate operations.

Three main elements make up this picture — a suitable setting for the subject; the lifelike presentation of wild or semidomestic birds, in the groupings and positions that they assume in such a setting; and, in order to give the birds sufficient prominence for them to be the subject of the picture, rather than details in a landscape, views of some of the birds from sufficiently close up to show some detail of coloring and pattern.

The setting was painted from studies of former gravel pits, which have filled with water and provided a magnificent reserve for many species of birds. The place is so extensive that details have been moved together to provide a more compact background, retaining the vivid and varied autumn colors. The groupings of the flocks of birds were also seen in the waterfowl reserve, most of them too far off for detailed study. The birds in the foreground — the mallard and Chinese geese — were drawn and studied from close quarters in an urban park. Care was taken when transferring them to the wilder setting to place them so that they were the right size to fit into it naturally.

Masking fluid was used on the swans, the rear parts of the geese, and the distant birds.

Bird house and garden

Original size: 14¼ × 21¼ in. (358 × 530 mm)
Paper: Mold-made Whatman 140 lb. (300 gsm)

Perhaps the most numerous and most easily observed of all the wild creatures that live in our gardens and streets are the garden birds that can be attracted to bird houses and windowsills. They are of course nervous and easily scared, but they can be watched from inside a room, so long as one stands hidden by a curtain, or far enough inside the room to be able to work without one's movements being seen. It is useful to keep a drawing board, paper, and pencil always ready so that when birds come to the bird house you can start drawing them immediately. Do not be discouraged if it seems difficult; it is amazing how soon it becomes easier as your knowledge increases and you become familiar with more species of birds. These drawings can then be used to compose a comparatively large and complicated picture, such as the one on these two pages.

The wall and border of flowers and shrubs are designed to provide a colorful backdrop for the main theme of the picture — the bird house, with its water dish, string of nuts, and half-coconut, and the different kinds of birds on it and around it. The area of grass has deliberately been left featureless to provide a background for the small figures of the birds, one that would not compete with or obscure them.

The dark cypresses at the back of the picture are similarly treated to enclose the right end of the picture; the flower border does this on the left. The cypresses also balance the dark green of the rosebush on the left.

Animal portraits

Now that we have come to the last page of the book, I hope that what I have written and demonstrated has shed some light on the problems of painting animals and pets in watercolor. I hope, too, that your enthusiasm has grown, and also your confidence in your ability to embark on an admittedly taxing but nevertheless rewarding subject, full of interest and variety. What is most important is to approach every painting as one that is totally different from any done in the past. When you paint an animal, you are in effect painting a portrait, with the same obligations of careful consideration and understanding of the subject as with a human portrait.

Every individual animal is a little different from the rest of its species, just as every individual Homo sapiens is a little different from any other. It is, however, necessary to be familiar with the variety to be able to recognize the differences. It has often been said, as though the fact suggested some mysterious power, that a shepherd can tell each sheep in his flock from all the others. But it is not considered remarkable for a schoolteacher to be able to tell one boy from another, or for a television watcher to distinguish between actors — we even recognize actors in disguise, and these are people we may never have seen in the flesh.

There is no mystery — if you are in a room with two dogs of the same breed, or two short-haired black cats, and start to draw them, you will immediately begin to see the differences between the two, and soon they will become two individuals to you. If you try the same thing with sheep, you will see differences between them, too. As long as you maintain an attitude of interested inquiry, every subject you embark on will be new and different, and you will have found a source of unending pleasure and fascination.